DATE DUE			
JAN 2 0 1981			
MAR 2 1 1984			
OCT 3 0 1994			
AUG 9 1986			
JUL 1 2 1988			
MAR 1 8 1992			
OCT 0 5 1996			

Weaving a Navajo Blanket

by

GLADYS A. REICHARD

DOVER PUBLICATIONS, INC.

New York

Published in Canada by General Publishing Company, Ltd., 30 Lesmill Road, Don Mills, Toronto, Ontario.
Published in the United Kingdom by Constable and Company, Ltd., 10 Orange Street, London WC 2.

This Dover edition, first published in 1974, is an unabridged and unaltered republication of the work originally published by J. J. Augustin, Publisher, New York in 1936 under the title *Navajo Shepherd and Weaver*.

International Standard Book Number: 0-486-22992-0
Library of Congress Catalog Card Number: 73-86437

Manufactured in the United States of America
Dover Publications, Inc.
180 Varick Street
New York, N.Y. 10014

To the memory of
Maria Antonia

Table of Contents

Illustrations

[ix]

Text figures

Acknowledgments

I was afforded the opportunity to learn Navajo weaving through the generosity of the Council for Research in the Social Sciences, Columbia University, and of the Southwest Society, and to them my initial thanks are due. I have mentioned in the Foreword my debt to Red Point's family and other Navajo teachers. I accord gratitude also to Hastin Gani's Wife, Mrs. Nanaba Bryan, Della Digrote, Eleanor Curley, and many other weavers whose names I do not know who have taught me by letting me watch them.

For aid of such various kinds that it often becomes intangible, being measured in terms of coöperation, stimulation, hints, and willingness to take no end of trouble in my behalf, I make deepfelt acknowledgment to the following: All connected with the J. L. Hubbell Trading Post, and especially to Mr. Roman Hubbell for introducing me to Red Point's family; all connected with the Crownpoint Trading Co., and especially to Mr. Lloyd Ambrose and Mr. Horace Boardman for photographs and sketches; Mr. and Mrs. Arthur F. Newcomb; Mr. and Mrs. B. I. Staples; Mr. Robert Karigan, and Mr. Hugh Bryan.

To the following who rendered expert advice and criticism in their respective fields, I am greatly indebted: Dr. B. Youngblood who criticised the chapter on Wool; Dr. L. C. Wyman and his colleagues, Drs. Harris and Walker, of Boston University for information on plants and chemistry; Mr. Edwin Eckel of the U. S. Geological Survey for advice on minerals. Although I greatly appreciate the services these friends rendered, in no case do I hold anyone but myself responsible for the interpretations and deductions made in this book.

My thanks extend to the following institutions for active and prompt coöperation: the Southwest Laboratory; the Museum of the American Indian, Heye Foundation; the American Museum of Natural History, and the Metropolitan Museum, all of which put all their facilities at my disposal. The American Museum of Natural History and the Metropolitan Museum furnished photographs also. I am grateful to McClurg and Co. of Chicago for permission to use the reproduction of the Little Weaver, from James', INDIAN BLANKETS AND THEIR MAKERS.

At the present time dye-history of the Navajo is in the making and Mr. Harrod, of Wells and Richardson, furnished me an unlimited supply of dyes for experimentation, as well as numerous suggestions regarding dyes. At my request he had developed the dyes now called "rust" and "tan" which are meant to match certain odd shades made ordinarily with natural dyes.

Barnard College, Gladys A. Reichard
Columbia University.

Foreword

This description of Navajo weaving aims to present the attitude of the weaver toward her work. It is based upon the experience of four summers (1930—1933) during which time I lived with Red Point's family and learned, among many other things, the principles of weaving. I myself tried all the processes described, with the constant, kindly, and patient critical accompaniment of my Navajo friends, and accomplished them with varying degrees of success.

Since the learning was empirical and as nearly like that of a Navajo as possible, it is to be expected that it was detailed. The only thing I knew when I started was that I was to transform wool into a Navajo blanket, and the theoretical principles of that transformation. The Navajo method of teaching is "showing"; never is there an explanation or a generalization. Most weavers do not analyze their problems, although a few can formulate their difficulties. They do, however, work out solutions which are sometimes novel and clever.

There is a great difference between experience with carding, spinning, weaving and just knowing about them or watching someone else do them. Experience points out the problems, suggests the motives, accepts or discards the procedures. All these depend upon knowledge and feeling for the smallest details and coördination of that information into a unit of action. Practise accomplishes this better than anything else.

Although the method may at first seem time-consuming, its rewards are of such a different nature from those obtained by any other method that they are well worth the time required. Besides showing up every weakness, it also furnished examples of individual cases, for every teacher has her peculiarities, and every weaver has her short-cuts. If one learns each move himself, he becomes aware of all departures from what he might define as the norm. At the same time he learns a great many things not directly connected with the weaving itself but quite as important to the ethnologist. Especially is this true of a group of people as isolated and scattered as any particular Navajo family.

On the other hand, it would be inefficient and foolish to rely on "showing" exclusively. It would mean that too much is left to chance. At Red Point's I learned the common type of weaving. Had I depended upon his women only, I should have remained ignorant of the saddleblanket weaves which are the most interesting forms of Navajo weaving, and which furnish as well the clues to its history. Here, as for other information, literature and generalization were valuable. Matthews[1] had recorded the fact of some of the saddleblanket weaves.

In recent years, the traders, Lloyd Ambrose and Horace Boardman, have been instrumental not only in reviving these complicated weaves, but also in disseminating an understanding of them with its attendant cultivation of taste in a discriminating buying public. They had collected and summarized these weaves; they had a collection of them on unfinished looms. They put their facilities at my disposal, and some hours of study in the blanket-room were supplemented by lessons with weavers who specialize in the particular types. Among them were the wife of Kinni's-Son, Juan's Wife and Della's Grandmother. After I had learned to make all these blankets in the vicinity of Thoreau, New Mexico, I returned to Red Point's to be told that Maria Antonia knew all but one kind. They are not popular where she lived but she had learned how to make them.

A second time my efficiency was increased when I learned that Mrs. Laura Armer had worked on the natural dyes. She did not know

---

[1] Matthews, W. Navajo Weavers. Report Bureau of American Ethnology, 3: 371—391.
—— A two-faced Navajo Blanket. American Anthropologist, n. s., 2 (1900): 638—642.

all the formulas herself but she knew an Indian who did, and he saved me a great deal of time. The process of making natural dyes is simple enough and is known to most Navajo in a general way, but the specific products needed to concoct the dyes are scarce and difficult to find. My interpreter and I spent several weeks and covered many miles of the Reservation in procuring them; we were able to make all the dyes I learned in only a few days.

Besides the advantage of unstinted aid and interest from the Navajo and many of the Whites of the Southwest, I have had the privilege of examining many Navajo blankets in museums and private collections. Although the present study is more concerned with the weaver and the way she makes her blanket than in the product of her loom, it is impossible to consider one without the other. Museums and blanket-rooms of traders have been invaluable in furnishing generalizations on the Navajo rug and blanket; they provide the initial clue to the why and wherefore.

With all this material at my disposal I have used also all the extant literature on Navajo weaving. I refer to it only sparingly in this work because I checked every statement at first hand. After I had been working at Red Point's for three summers, I learned that Mr. Charles Amsden was also making a study of Navajo weaving.

Fortunately he was interested in the subject from that point of view in which my interest was weakest. He writes of the blanket for its own sake and particularly for the history, not only of Navajo weaving, but of all weaving in America. His account[1] appeared at the end of 1933 when the results of my own study had been written but not published. Since Mr. Amsden's report is complementary to this one, and since the point of view is so different, I am indicating with brackets and notes such remarks as I added after reading his book. Few enough, they are by way of discussion, in several cases, of dis-

[1] Amsden, Charles Avery. Navaho Weaving. The Fine Arts Press, Santa Ana, California, 1934.

agreement with his conclusions, and of answer to some of the questions he leaves open.

My purpose in discussing the technique of Navajo weaving in this form has been twofold: first, to present the weaver's viewpoint; and second, to enable anyone with the will, to learn to weave a Navajo blanket. A friend of mine made a much more presentable rug than my first attempt from the description before photographs and drawings were available.

I *The Weaver*

I learned to weave blankets while living with a Navajo family at a place on the Reservation called White Sands. The head of the family is Red Point. This old patriarch, with his wife Maria Antonia, occupied the central hogan (house) of his little settlement. Each of their three daughters had their own hogans nearby. One daughter, Marie, and her husband, Tom Curley, were my interpreters and teachers when they were home. I lived in one of the houses at Red Point's for four summers, during the second of which Marie and Tom were in Los Angeles. By this time I was able to speak enough Navajo to get along and Red Point's older daughter, Atlnaba, was my teacher.

I wanted to know how the Navajo women feel about their craft, how they themselves learn, how they teach and criticise. I have described their attitudes toward their work and toward me in an informal personal account, entitled *Spider Woman*[1]. It is a tale of digressions. Preparation of yarn and the weaving itself are activities always on hand; only rarely, in the summer at least, do the women make a business of them. If the family needs the money secured for the rugs, if one of the women is a recognized artist, if circumstances are such that her labor may be spared from other necessary pursuits, she may be given the leisure to weave and is required to do little else. All these conditions are filled in only a few cases.

Most commonly all stages of the process from carding to weaving are in progress. A woman may have two, or even three rugs started. She will stop weaving to cook or superintend the flock, sometimes even to herd, if no young or old people are available. It is not the province of a successful Navajo matron to herd, but if necessity demands she will do it. She can take her spinning, especially of warp, with her if she must tend the sheep all day.

[1] The Macmillan Co., 1934.

Even the home-maker is often interrupted. In the early summer she spends a part of each day in the corn-patch carefully coaxing the crops to withstand the dry winds and the cutting sands. Later, if her efforts have been successful, she works for days preserving the corn for winter by roasting and drying. Some days she will have visitors. At such times all may card or spin, or the hostess may quietly twist her own yarn as she sits and talks. Her weaving may be further hindered by her attendance at the ever-present "sings", religious rituals which vary all the way from an apparent social diversion with hundreds, even thousands, of guests to the most serious of emergency measures witnessed only by the members of the immediate family.

The purpose of a "sing" is curative or prophylactic, to cure an ailment or to prevent one. One may be held if a person suddenly becomes ill, or an individual who is slightly ailing may join with others who plan to hold a rite in order to procure for himself a blessing and protection from future evil. In either case the weaver may be present, in the capacity of patient, cook, or guest.

Once or twice a year the entire family moves for some days for the sheep dipping, a job which requires the efforts of old and young. It means that our weaver must remain away from home at least two or three days at the dipping, not counting the time it takes her to go and come. There is never any hurry about all this. Although the work is hard, it is done in a lively holiday spirit, as is most Navajo work. The dippers see acquaintances they have not seen for a long time, they meet new ones, they gossip and laugh. On the way home the weaver may stop at the store and trade for an afternoon, or she may visit one of her friends for several days.

The story of "my family" is one which records the responsibility Red Point's women took for me from the moment I arrived until the present time. A Navajo rarely commits himself to responsibility for a white man but once he does, it is as binding as his duty to his own, or so at least I found it. Maria Antonia and her daughters undertook to teach me to weave. Never once in the four summers I spent with them was their duty forsworn. Every sign of progress I made was a source of pride as great to them as to me. At the end of the fourth summer I learned that at first they had been as worried that they might not be able to teach me, as I was that I might not be able to learn. Since, however, they were not as much in a hurry as I was, and since my progress was immediate and steady, their apprehension was short-lived.

The Navajo word for "teach" is to "show", and that is exactly what they do. These women, "my grandmother and sisters", showed me, with unfailing patience and persistent good humor, each step in the long process of transforming wool from a sheep's back to the rug with complicated design accepted by the trader. At first I had to learn a dozen things at once, for tapestry weaving is a matter of coördination. My instructors laughed at my awkwardness, sympathized with my injuries, corrected my mistakes, criticised my results. They were never harsh in their criticism but they never allowed an error to pass un-noticed. They always kept me up to the highest standards.

During the period of my apprenticeship I was taught specific things. I mastered a great many details, no one of which may be omitted in the experience of a good weaver. With a few exceptions I learned as a Navajo girl learns to weave. My teaching differed from hers in inten-sity and concentration, and possibly in materials. Children learning to weave may be given scraps for their materials. I always had the best.

I have already told the story of the way Atlnaba and Marie learned to weave.[1] Atlnaba wanted to weave when she was less than four years old. An older sister, Adjiba, allowed her to work a little on the blankets she was weaving and by the time Atlnaba was five (Pl. I, a)[2] she was weaving blankets accepted by the trader. She followed a course quite

[1] Spider Woman, Chap. VI.
[2] The caption used by James "Tuli, the Child Weaver" is a mistake.

usual with Navajo children. She began with the last process, that of weaving, and gradually picked up expertness in the preparation of her materials and in making her loom after she had mastered the weaving itself. Her sister had given her good materials and at first she had no need to construct her loom.

By the time Marie, who was three years younger than Atlnaba, wanted to weave, Adjiba had died. Maria Antonia did not want the child to spoil her blanket by experimentation, she was not patient enough to teach her little daughter; furthermore, she wanted Marie to herd and the two activities are incompatible. Marie's desire was so strong, however, that she made her own loom and implements from such materials as she could procure, and bit by bit filched enough yarn from her mother to enable her to set up a tiny loom which she took with her each time she drove the sheep off to graze.

These two children exemplify the two extremes of training girls to weave. Atlnaba with all materials of the best, no loom to construct, and the gentle guidance of her older sister, learned quickly. At five her success was spectacular; it took many more years for her to become expert at the fundamental, but more prosaic, tasks which white men scarcely notice. Marie learned to weave in spite of her environment rather than because of it. She had to make her comb, batten and loom. Because she could take only a small quantity of her mother's yarn at a time, she had to learn from the very beginning to splice the separate pieces. Her achievement was accomplished to the accompaniment of tears, undaunted perseverance, and wrathful fits of discouragement. When complete, there was for her no glory, no approval, no praise, for she hung her first three blankets on a tree, where they could be seen only by the birds which pulled at their loose strings and by the sheep which shied at their flapping in the wind.

Many women are proud when their little daughters start to weave and encourage them by giving them good yarn and by "showing" them how to go about it. Usually the children make their own looms instead of working on those of their mothers. A small blanket, far better than my first one, brought to a trader, was said to have been made by a child three and one-half years old. She must have had much help, but even so I cannot conceive how her tiny hands had the strength to manage the healds even though they had the coördination. I believe the statement, even though I do not comprehend it, for I once saw Djiba, when she was only two and one-half — she has always been small for her age — fill a bowl six inches in diameter and four deep with water from a coffee pot twice as heavy. Three times she raised the full bowl from the ground to her lips without spilling a drop. Skill like this is possible although it seems incredible.

My learning was like Atlnaba's. I had good materials and implements, willing and patient teachers, and I started at the final process so that results were not too far distant. I have learned all the other steps necessary to preparation of the yarn and to the setting up of the loom, but I am far from expert at some of them, in none have I attained the expertness of any one of my teachers. This is not surprising when I consider that Marie spun for nine years before she could pronounce her yarn "real good".

II *Wool*

The Navajo, particularly the women, are "sheep-minded". From the first white crack of dawn to the time when the curtain of darkness descends they must consider the sheep. Yes, and even beyond. For it is not unusual to wake at night to find the flock munching and belching just outside the hogan. A venturesome goat has nosed down a weak log of the corral, or has beaten a trail over the confines. The sheep, not original in blazing the trail, but gifted in imitating, have followed and made their way hoganwards. It is not necessary to get up and drive them back, but the owner sleeps with one ear open, and if they nibble their way out of hearing, it will save time and anxiety to drive them back.

What is this animal the thought of which occupies their waking and even sleeping moments? The origin of the Navajo sheep, like that of most of our valued domesticated animals, is really unknown. There is much speculation about it, but after all is said and done, the actual facts which survive a careful sifting are few. Two periods of influence must be recognized. The first may be called the pre-Ft. Sumner period during which the Navajo herded sheep on a comparatively small scale for their own use. It is possible that the breed of this period was related to the type described for the early French in Louisiana and Texas. It is, however, of little significance as far as the present-day sheep are concerned, for the imprisonment of the Navajo at Ft. Sumner for four years marked a dividing line at which some phases of Navajo life ended and others began. Such few sheep as may have survived from that early period would probably have had so little effect on the huge flocks of the present day as to be negligible.

The term "sheep" as used by the Navajo includes a great many features. We might perhaps speak of "sheep which the Navajo have" and "the Navajo sheep". The types belonging to the first category are practically limitless because they are constantly changing. There are white sheep with long hair, white sheep with wavy hair, black sheep, brown sheep, brown with black spots, black with brown spots, grayish brown sheep and brownish gray. As is true for the Navajo dogs, no combination seems impossible. The flocks will differ, too, according to the part of the Reservation where they roam, for the various districts have been influenced by as many theories of "improvement" as there are white men interested in them.

By "Navajo sheep" is meant a peculiar breed, the origin of which is mixed, but which is the favorite of the Navajo, especially of the weaver. It owes its survival to its smallness, and its resistance to hunger, thirst and sudden changes in weather, particularly temperature. Its smallness is no drawback in the Navajo mind and the toughness of the meat is, in his opinion, an advantage. He believes that tough meat is more sustaining than tender. So firm is this conviction that, not only is meat used shortly after killing, but it is intentionally prevented from long boiling. The Navajo say, "It seems like you are getting more to eat if the meat is tough."

The fleece of the Navajo sheep is light, averaging only about two and a half to four pounds as compared to an average of six to sixteen pounds of other sheep and even twenty-five to thirty of the Rambouillet. Its lightness is, however, of small moment to the weaver when she considers its other qualities, the character of the staple, and the relative freedom from grease. The staple is long and wavy in contrast to the merino and Rambouillet strains which have been introduced into the Navajo flocks, at first accidentally, later with the idea of consciously improving the wool and meat standards. The merino wool derives its popularity from its crimpiness, a quality which permits a heavier fleece than a straight or merely wavy hair. For marketing purposes a heavy fleece is desirable, for hand-carding and spinning, extreme crimpiness may be a severe handicap, for the craftsman must achieve with primitive implements and hand power that which our

[7]

own wool manufacturers attain by means of complicated machinery run by electricity.

The black sheep of Navajo flocks has the crimpiness of the merino and no amount of carding, or skill in hand-spinning will create a smooth yarn comparable to that which is easily achieved from the white Navajo fleece. The wool from the Navajo sheep is relatively free from grease, a desirable quality in wool which is to be hand-carded. In the old literature it is said that the Navajo used to take special pains to keep their sheep from acquiring merino blood so as to prevent the wool from becoming oily and crimpy.

A white friend of mine who has been weaving for many years, who has learned many weaves of our white civilization, and who has experimented widely with different kinds of wool, avers that the Navajo wool I have, with all its burrs and sand, is freer from oil before it is carded than the English wools she has used after they have been hand-washed five times.

For many years numerous movements have been aimed at the improvement of Navajo herds. They have been disinterested to only a limited extent, but the general theory is that what will benefit the white man will help the Indian too. Even the worthiest motives have been based upon misunderstandings and ignorance, or perhaps ignoring, of actual conditions, which are primarily geographic. Since the merino and the French merino or Rambouillet were good types for Europeans and for us, the Navajo were urged to breed for the qualities these sheep possessed — qualities, of course, in a white man's market.

Besides the disadvantages of the wool for weaving, the sheep bred from these parents have an additional handicap in their struggle for survival. The very weight of the much-folded fleece and its oiliness combine to hinder its wearer. Such a fleece, heavy enough in itself, gathers up all sorts of impedimenta present on a desert range. The herbs of the mesas, concerned with the same contest with drought as

[8]

the sheep, have many prickles, briars, burrs and such excrescences which stick to the fleece and cannot be rubbed or shaken free easily. The oil of the pelt causes sand and dust to adhere for a long time. Consequently, the animal with the "desirable" fleece is carrying about with it much greater weight than is necessary. The result is that it is slower than its less highly pedigreed mates and must take the leftovers in pasturage when it at last reaches them.

It would be difficult, if not impossible, for a Navajo to sum up the disadvantages of the "better" breeds in this way, so for many years he said nothing, but quietly though firmly resisted the "improving" of his flocks. On the eastern side of the Lukachukai Mountains, however, sheep have been highly bred for weight of flesh and wool, the aim being to sell in the world market. Indeed, the policy has been so thoroughly followed in one locality that now very little, if any, Navajo wool is woven. For such weaving as is done, carded wool bought from the trader is used. The Navajo at this place have reached such "an end to a circle" as we ourselves are capable of.

But in the more "backward" regions of the Reservation where Navajo still live by their own efforts, the women have something to say about sheep breeding. They want wool, good wool, for weaving. They therefore select for their own work that from the "oldtime Navajo" sheep. I have seen wool of this kind so clean and long that it could be spun without carding. This is not a common occurrence, however.

A real improvement in Navajo flocks must be based upon an intelligent survey of what the breeding is done for. Let us assume, as some estimate, that ten percent of the wool is woven at home by the Navajo women. That is an important ten percent because it furnishes not only the cash resources of the family, but it is also the satisfaction of their creative ability. Twenty percent of the flocks is sold for meat, and twenty percent more is depended on for wool to sell; and at the same time that dealers demand flesh, they demand good pelts, and the qualifications for both go hand in hand. The problem thus becomes

[9]

the age-old one of a close-to-the-soil, handcraft type of mind struggling to compete with modern business and manufacturing methods. From our point of view forty percent of the number of sheep is an overwhelming argument in favor of improvement of flesh and fleece, but we are not Navajo who like tough meat and who weave. Furthermore, we have never driven a flock through the sagebrush of the Navajo country. Sheep herding is sufficiently trying without having to drive hundreds of extra pounds of countryside clinging to heavy, folded pelts. In the Navajo's place I believe I should choose to cultivate flocks of "good rustlers" rather than flocks of money-getters. I can eat them and my wife can weave the wool even if there is less of it.

More recently there are new elements in breeding. Experimentation is going on in a limited way with Corriedale rams introduced into flocks of the old Navajo sheep. The Corriedale is a New Zealand breed of sheep which produces good mutton and wool. Besides, the animals are hardy and good foragers. The wool contains little oil and is longer than that of the Navajo sheep, having a looser crimp than the Rambouillet. The results at crossing so far obtained seem to be desirable. It is possible that the introduction of the Corriedale strain might solve the major difficulties of the Navajo problem.[1]

In considering such unsatisfactory statistics as we have for Navajo enterprise one is tempted to offer the following solution: Since the the Navajo weave only ten percent of their wool why do they not breed a certain number of animals for their own weaving supply, the old type if need be, and improve the rest of their flocks? The question leaves out the Navajo personal equation. He does not keep his flocks

[1] This study of weaving was made before the numerous investigations of the Department of Indian Affairs began in 1933. At that time almost complete control of Navajo range conditions was placed in the hands of the Soil Erosion Control division of the Department of Agriculture working with the Department of the Interior, and conditions have changed so rapidly and so frequently that it would be much beyond the scope of this study to evaluate this movement, even if the writer felt any assurance of her ability to do so, which she does not. It will suffice to say that the changes wrought by these agencies have become nothing short of cataclysmic.

separate. He may try to breed for wool, but if he does his whole flock will be bred that way. He does not, perhaps cannot, keep flocks separate. The solution of his problem must be a compromise between the ten percent and the forty percent; it cannot be a good resolving of ten percent and forty percent as such.

The increase in the goat population in recent years is an outgrowth of Navajo reasoning. Goats were at first introduced because they have more sense than sheep and therefore are easier to herd. They lead and the sheep follow. They are hardy, too, able to exist on forage too high, too rough or too acrid for sheep. The Navajo like goat meat as well as mutton. The so-called "mohair" sometimes brings a better price than wool. The women have learned to make excellent yarn of mohair and the rugs they weave from it are beyond criticism technically and artistically. Mohair is more difficult to spin but rugs woven of it bring higher prices and outwear wool ones.

The one argument against goat raising concerns the long-view of the Navajo future. The country has already changed its aspect considerably within the memory of man. The explanation given by rangers and water men is that it is over-grazed. The sheep eat off the grass to a low level, but not so low that the roots cannot survive. The goats eat it so close that it never recovers. Moreover, they eat off the leafage of the higher herbs, and even the low branches of trees, so close and so frequently that much of the vegetation is utterly destroyed. The ranger argues that the devastation caused by running washes and the cutting up of the country is due to the denudation of the soil. There are no roots to hold the sand when it is attacked by the heavy sudden showers of the rainy season. The Navajo does not understand this. Call his attention to the fact that there was, even within his memory, plenty of grass where now there is none and he answers, "It is because the Navajo do not live as they used to. They do not follow the teaching of the gods. Girls marry men of their own clan, people go to doctors instead of having sings. We ought to live like we did in old times."

Dipping the Sheep

Dipping the herds to prevent and cure scabies and other pests with which the animals may become infected is an annual occurrence. When I first went into the Navajo country in 1923, the flocks were badly affected. Besides, the Navajo did not understand that *one* scraggly sheep could infect the whole flock. During my short visit I saw at two places portions of the flock which their owners "held out on the sheep dippers". They had sent the large majority to the dip, but these dozen or so had been near where lightning struck and could not go until they were ceremonially released from the contamination due to the elements. That would not be until the men came back from the dipping, which meant these animals were not dipped at all.

By dint of much education and some coercion the "sheep men" now succeed in getting most of the sheep dipped. Their improved methods are more convincing to the Navajo. Formerly they used only a nicotine solution. It was found to be effective in some regions and useless in others. Experiment showed that the difference was due to the water. Where it is soft the nicotine reacts favorably, where hard, there is no result. The rangers then tried out a sulphur solution which is useful in all kinds of water. The sulphur is not as dangerous to the sheep. Dipping is a task demanding skill. The sheep must be thoroughly immersed for the head is a seat of infection, but if the medicine gets in the eyes or throat of the animal it may become ill or die according to the amount it imbibes. The loss entailed in sulphur dipping is greatly lessened as compared with nicotine.

It was found that scabies could be more thoroughly eradicated if treatment were repeated within a ten-day period. In 1933 the Navajo were required to dip the sheep twice within that period of time. There was considerable grumbling about this, but no active opposition. As a result the flocks in many districts are now almost free of the pest. They were dipped in 1934 only once as a preventive measure.

The attitude at Ganado (and I suppose in other districts also) is one of pride, satisfaction at having eradicated the pest, and complacency at having mastered a new skill. Very few sheep are lost through the dipping. Red Point's family lost none in two summers. The mortality depends almost entirely upon the dippers. Some are "rough", that is, inhumane or careless. The women particularly are influential in curbing the men at work. They choose those for their own flocks whom they know to be trustworthy; they watch the dipping carefully; they do not hesitate to help in the hard work it involves.

Shearing

The first step in the conversion of wool is shearing, which is done in the early spring. The wool is then thick because it is a winter fleece. The natives wait until the weather is warm enough so that the sheep will not suffer. The wool crop, like all others, depends upon the season. If the season is early, it may be sheared before it has become thin and uneven. If the season is late, as it was in 1933, the crop is poor. The sheep run about rubbing against brush and rocks; it is the natural time for moulting and the delay, while helpful to the sheep, spells heavy loss for its owner.

The shearer ties the legs of each animal together, places it before her and with ordinary hand-shears proceeds systematically to clip the fleece from neck to tail. The Navajo makes no effort to keep the fleece in one piece although a skilful worker may do so. There is no particular selection of wool as in our own elaborate process of mechanical manufacture, but the weaver chooses her weaving wool from the back of the Navajo sheep, never from the neck or the belly. The wool is best at the shoulders and side of the animal. The quality becomes coarser toward the tail. The wool on the belly and front of the throat is short, worn and dirty, and that on the head and shins is short, stiff and straight, more like hair.

According to all the published accounts this would be the place to give directions for washing the wool. The descriptions are given on the basis of the way our grandmothers and the Europeans from whom they learned treated their wool. On only one occasion, when Atlnaba was experimenting with dyes, have I seen wool washed before it was spun. I have asked every woman I have seen about the matter. All agree that washing wool is to be avoided if possible because it becomes tightly matted and lumpy, thus making it difficult to card. In rare cases it is too dirty to card, then it may be washed. More commonly, however, it is laid on a rock in the sun and vigorously beaten. Most weavers save themselves this trouble by carefully selecting clean, suitable wool before they send their surplus to market.

Carding

Carding is a process not generally understood by the layman. The end desired in making any kind of cordage is to secure a strong slender filament. Its achievement depends upon the regular and shapely combination of the fibers of which it is composed. Whatever the material composing the necessary yarn may be, it must assume its final form by passing through a series of processes each of which arranges the fibers in some order more nearly approaching the end product. Wool as it comes from the sheep's back is a matted, dirty, irregular mass. Automatically as she works, the weaver pulls the mat apart as she chooses the small bits for her towcards. She fluffs it slightly with her fingers and at the same time picks out the most noticeable foreign materials. She then lays the fluff upon one of her towcards.

There is some evidence, though very slight, which hints that the Navajo may have known weaving in prehistoric times. There is none,

PLATE I

[a]
Atlnaba, the child weaver (courtesy McClurg and Co.)

[b]
A good edge

[c]
Edge of double-faced blanket

PLATE II

[a]
Carding

[b]
Carding

[d]
First spinning

[e]
Pulling wool even

[c]
Position of spindle and splicing of laps

however, that they had ever worked out the idea of the towcards. They are a strong arrangement whereby teeth of some sort may be attached. In Europe teazels were used for the sharp teeth. There were plants in the Navajo territory which would have served the purpose nicely. The Spanish who first came into the Southwest used a towcard of this sort [illustrated by Amsden, Pl. 10. It is impossible to tell from the illustration whether or not iron nails were used. They would not be absolutely necessary. At best the device is of such a complicated nature that the Navajo without fine tools and with no development of the art of wood carving would not have had the facilities to make it].

The carding implements used by the Navajo were doubtless all of Spanish provenience. Those used today have metal teeth set into an elastic foundation. They are sold by all traders on the Reservation. Traders and weavers alike complain about their flimsiness. The work of carding is simple but it requires great muscular strength and endurance. The pressure applied by strong arms must be resisted firmly by the cards. The towcards sold today do not stand the strain long and soon the teeth bend or come out altogether.

The main object of carding is to arrange the wool fibers evenly so that they may be spun. Since European hand-weavers wash their wool first, this is their only purpose. The Navajo weaver uses her cards for an additional effect. Water is almost non-existent in her grazing lands; such as there is must be kept almost exclusively for internal use. Her sheep are consequently not washed before shearing, but since the wool is not oily, beating, pulling or pressure will cause the sand and other undesirable objects to fall out. The regular persistent friction of the towcards, together with some aid from the fingers, leaves the wool several hundred times as clean as it was originally.

Carding is a task which is hard on the hands especially if the wool filaments are crimpy. It takes strength and the position of the hands is an unusual, cramped one. Besides, the work is dirty. I know of no woman who fancies carding as a pastime. Often a group of women get together and card a large amount of wool at one time so that they will not have to do it again for some time.

Mohair is advantageous at this stage, for the fibers are so straight that little carding suffices to bring them into order. The ideal combination is that of mohair and wool. The mohair adds to the ease of carding; the wool supplies the friction necessary to make the desirable felt.

The wool of the Navajo black sheep is never as fine or regular as that of the white. Often it is very crimpy indeed. It takes longer to card black and the resulting laps have small crimpy tufts which no amount of carding can eliminate.

"Sheep gray", which is more nearly tan, is selected from the back of the yellowish brown sheep. Since it is a natural color, the carding is the same as for white or black. A real gray is used much more extensively than "sheep gray". Its shade is secured by carding. The worker lays a portion of white and a wad of black between her cards and tries to mix them evenly. She uses more of one color or the other according as she wants the shade dark or light. As she proceeds she matches, as nearly as her judgment allows, the lap she is carding to those she has just finished.

The weaving of sandpainting tapestries demands unusual shades such as pink or light green. Some careful weavers, instead of dyeing white in a dilute red dye-bath, dye white uncarded wool red, then mix it with white in carding. Although this requires more labor, the result has a softness which could not otherwise be obtained. Colors like pink and light green are used only sparingly, and if a weaver is going to the trouble of weaving a sandpainting at all, she is not likely to mind a little additional effort.

III *Yarn*

After the wool is carded, the spinner begins her work. She takes half of the rectangular pad which has left the towcards, moistens one end and causes it to adhere loosely to the end of her spindle. This she can do at once if she has the knack, otherwise the wool will slip off the spinning stick several times before she has it under control. The skill consists in securing an exact relationship between the tension at which the wool is held in the left hand, the twirl of the stick (reasonably fast), and the angle the wool makes with the stick. After it has been made to cling, a nice balance must be kept between the twirling stick and the drawing wool.

The base of the spindle whirs on the ground at the right of the spinner, if she is right-handed (Pl. II, *c*). The upper end of the stick rests lightly on the inside of her right thumb with all four fingers over it. As she twirls it toward her with a rhythmic alternation of thumb and first and second fingers it slides freely back and forth from the end of her thumb to its base.

The wool is regulated by the spinner's left hand. It is held between her thumb and first finger, the palm of the hand turned up. She presses her thumb firmly against her index finger in order to pull the staple as tight as it needs to be held. The drawing resolves itself into a contest between a slightly jerking pull combined with the turn of the spindle downward and a firm stretch, as evenly distributed as possible, of the wool upward. The ideal is a loose twist of yarn about the thickness of a middle finger, an even twist as tight and as loose here as there.

When the first half of the pad is in this shape the second half must be spliced to it. There is a trick to this also, based on securing the twist at the end of the spindle stick, a twist which involves a smooth union of the end staples of each half pad. By the time these two processes which are nearly alike — one involves keeping the wool on the spindle, the other wool adhering to wool — are mastered, the spinning lesson is nearly learned. There is a whorl, usually wooden, a few inches from the base of the spindle. It serves to weight the stick so as to give it momentum and keeps the twisted wool from sliding off. The aim of the first spinning is to get the wool into a continuous strand which is like a thick fluffy rope with a loose twist (Pl. II, *d*). As the wool takes on its roll-like shape it is wound about the lower part of the spindle.

Spinning, like a few other things, cannot be taught. A woman can "show" me how to do it; I must learn the coördination through practise. The perfection of the art is one which depends largely on feeling, a niceness of balance and judgment between implement, material, and the spinner's hands. The first wool will come off lumpy, thick and loose at one place, thin and tight at another. There will be difficulty in splicing and often the strand will tear. It is more difficult to splice where the wool has torn than where two raw ends are placed together. The beginner will hold her wool close to her spindle. She learns through observation and experimentation that the farther away from the stick she is able to hold it, the greater will be the distance through which the stretch can operate. She will know then that a little stretch over a long distance will result in greater uniformity than if that same stretch were taken up within a short space.

She will find also after more experience that the fibers of her wool are susceptible to an almost infinite amount of stretch and that they will withstand an extraordinary amount of strain. She will be surprised to find that, after what seems to be an incredible amount of abuse, they still hold together and firmly too. She also discovers that the resistance will be great only if the fibers are stretched and twisted at the proper angle. They must be pulled lengthwise, never sidewise. Practise and experience will overcome all her difficulties, but nothing else will. The learner will at first have to give her entire concentration

[*18*]

to her task, perhaps biting her tongue the while. Soon she will be talking and joking as her spinning continues. She will find now that her splices *are* spliced, and that her wool does not tear, but the result is lumpy and uneven. She will soon notice that each time she picks up her work the spun wool will be more uniform.

The spinner has a number of balls of bulky, fuzzy, lightly twisted wool wound in the loosest fashion, and begins her second spinning. She is preparing her ordinary weft yarn. She fastens the end of her loosely spun roll to her spindle stick and in exactly the same way as before, twirls it holding the thick soft roll in her left hand. She now has a great advantage, for unless she tears her fibers she does not need to splice often. Her spinning will progress smoothly and rapidly.

It is not difficult to understand why spinning has become famed in song and story, why poets extol the nobility of the spinner, why the art has even become symbolic of "goodness". Navajo spinning, at least, requires the simplest of materials. A spindle can always be carried with the little light wool necessary, even when a woman goes riding, or herding on foot. The simplicity of the art, combined with the grace necessary for skill, are sufficient to account for the sentimentality arising in the soul of him who does not spin, even if we leave out the admiration arising from the fact that he has tried and failed, or knows he would fail if he did try.

There are only slight differences in the manner of spinning kinds of yarn other than the ordinary weft yarn. The variation is in the tightness of the twist and the number of times a strand is spun. The most commonly used weft is spun only twice. The yarn used in "vegetable dye" blankets is much coarser and softer than that customarily used, but it is made in the same way with a looser twist. I have seen spinners match up their results with the thickness of yarn being used by the weaver for whom they are spinning. Because of the inequalities of fleece, gray and black yarns are always ruder than the white or bright colored ones, even though much effort is expended in their preparation. There are cases, not rare, where these irregularities make for considerable charm.

Mohair yarn, which is encouraged when goats are plentiful, is made in the same way but with greater difficulty. It is smooth, wiry, and straight as compared with wool. Although a crimpy wool is not desirable, a wave in the staple makes it easier to splice because it furnishes more of the necessary friction. It is only an expert spinner who has the patience and ability to spin the mohair. She must be willing also, like Maria Antonia, to make a physical sacrifice, for women who spin mohair say it wears their fingers almost "down to the bone".

The results, however, are the most satisfactory achievement of the modern blanket maker. The yarn is fine and even, as good as that in the best of the old rugs, and it takes on color readily and uniformly when dyed. Besides its excellent texture it has an artistic quality that cannot be overestimated. Even after spinning has twisted in the required fibers, there remain a number of long hairs along the edge of the yarn. When woven into a pattern these hairs serve to blend the contrasting colors softly, giving the design the same effect as is secured by printing photographs slightly out of focus.

When the spindle is full of weft yarn, the spinner winds it into a skein by passing it under the sole of her shoe or moccasin and over her bent knee, this distance fixing its length. When it is wound she makes a turn about the thickness of the skein and fastens it with a double strand loop by means of which it will hang until wound into a ball for use.

Warp made of mohair is smooth and practically indestructible. It is used only by the best craftsmen. Warp, whether of mohair or wool, may be spun as often as five times. Ordinarily it is spun only twice. It is always spun tighter and finer than weft so that its essential features are hardness and strength (Pl. III, *b*). There is nothing the spinner is more conscious of than the tremendous strain her warp will have to bear. She aims to make it resistant by the regularity and tightness of her spinning.

A combination of wool and mohair is now becoming popular for warp. The wool makes it easier to spin, the mohair furnishes additional strength and excellent texture.

The warp spinner can wind a large amount of the fine yarn on her spindle. When it is full she winds it off into a hard ball, carefully watching that the curls due to the tight twist do not become knotted. She does not wash her warp. She perhaps has made it of white which left something to be desired for purity, or even of a mixture of colors. The color does not matter. It is strong and even. The warp of a well woven rug does not show.

There is a great contrast between the old Navajo blankets and their modern counterparts. The difference is due to many factors, not the least of which is the yarn. One often remarks the softness of old rugs as compared with new ones. The cause of this softness is often just age, or better, wear. A modern rug which has been walked on for two or three years is far superior to a brand new one or to one that has never been used. Multiply the age by ten or fifteen and one understands easily the superiority, other factors being equal, of the older blankets.

Another element which added fineness to the earlier blankets was the additional care taken in smoothing the yarn. It was drawn, in some instances, across a corncob, in others over a piece of sandstone, to take off the fuzz and lumps which made it uneven. This process is still used by the Hopi and must be an old one, for even in prehistoric ruins sandstones grooved in the same way as a few modern ones are found in considerable numbers. Nowadays only the oldest and most careful workers smooth their yarn, except as it becomes smooth by careful selection of wool and expert spinning. Only twenty or thirty years ago all good weavers in the Ganado region used the smoothing process, today few indeed ever heard of it and practically none use it.

One of the secrets of the exquisite texture of Peruvian threads was the use of the principle of doubling, tripling, or quadrupling the ply. If an uneven thread is doubled and retwisted, the chances that a thick portion of one thread will come at a thin part of the other are good, the retwist will cause them to fit so snugly that a much smoother yarn results. The Navajo make two-, three-, and four-ply yarn but never use it for weaving, only for edges, bindings, or ropes.

Those blankets which catch at once the eye of the collector or connoisseur, those which are dated as fifty to two hundred years old, are really made of materials entirely different from those in use today. The blankets, numerous in collections — I do not wish at this point to discuss their age — are frankly made of non-Navajo wefts. They belong to that period of our own history when the Whites had standards of quality. Beauty and durability of fabric were appreciated, in fact demanded, by the frontier residents who came from Spain which was at that time the foremost wool-producing country of the world. This was the period during which many Navajo women were slaves (or servants) of the Whites of the Southwest and of northern Mexico. Strangely enough we have no examples of traditional stages in the rug making of the Navajo. Those examples which purport to be the oldest represent a fully developed technique.

The warp of some of the old blankets is the same as that of the modern ones. Some others have an excellent quality of four-ply wool warp. In others four-ply cotton warp, far superior to the cotton warp sometimes used today in inferior blankets, is used. These more-than-one-ply yarns were certainly importations for there is no evidence that the Navajo ever used the principle of doubling or tripling the weight of their spinnings for smoothness of texture.

The weft is often vari-colored and many-shaded of fine Germantowns and Saxonys. The color and texture of these were better than those of the same yarns used at the present time. There is no doubt that the Navajo accepted these yarns, then, as they do with everything,

[22]

adapted them to their own use by respinning and sometimes by re-coloring. Particularly was that true of the famous "bayetas", the most valuable of the old Navajo blankets. Since there is no general agreement as to the exact origin of these blankets, since most accounts of the Navajo blanket have lengthy discussions on bayeta, and since this is an account of the modern Navajo weaver, a mere reference to them will be adequate.

"Bayeta" was a woolen material imported by the Spanish and Mexicans of this country from Spain, which region imported it in turn from England where it is called "baize". It was sold by the yard directly to the Indians as late as 1920 at the J. Lorenzo Hubbell Trading Post at Ganado. Up to 1900 it was used quite extensively. The last bayeta blanket was brought into this post, unfinished, in 1912. The Navajo women ravelled the material secured by trade, and respun it. It seems more reasonable to suppose they did this to get a long continuous strand rather than because they were not satisfied with the texture.

Bayeta yarn thus respun is fine and even in twist. It has a long nap, is waterproof, and durable. It is almost impossible to wear it out. It was used in the days when the Navajo used the blankets themselves. The man who has a feeling for texture, and judgment based on experience in handling fabrics, will be able to distinguish bayeta yarn from other kinds. It has a sheen different from all other yarns and a peculiar wiriness which can be felt quite easily. Frequently a small quantity was used with other yarns. Not seldom an old blanket was woven with several inches of red bayeta and the rest of the weaving, even though the same color, of some other yarn. In the face of the exaggeration, especially of value, which is put on bayeta by collectors, it should not be forgotten that the contemporary Germantowns and Saxonys were yarns quite worthy of combination with the much lauded bayeta. If the Navajo weaver is left to her own devices, her mohair may become an acceptable substitute for bayeta, especially if age gives it an opportunity to "ripen".

IV Color

The yarn, in a family like Red Point's, hangs in many skeins from loomframes and protuberances of the hogan. A foresighted and enthusiastic weaver will be at least one ball of warp ahead of her weaving. Maria Antonia could always produce one from the innumerable sacks hanging from her shapeless shade. Atlnaba will have one hidden under a bag of wool or on a crosslog of her roof.

As soon as the size and design of the blanket have been determined the final preparation of the yarn is undertaken. The weaver makes a mental estimate of the amount of each color necessary. She will need more of the background color than of any other shade. Suppose her background is gray and she is going to introduce a black, white and red design. Atlnaba, expert that she is, will have matched her gray carefully when she carded it so that she will have only to reckon on having enough. She will keep separate her "sheep gray" and her "carded gray". One of her specialties is a tan gray, "sheep gray", which she uses for sandpainting backgrounds. She does not have enough of the natural wool, but supplements her yarn by carding black and white together.

She estimates that she needs for this ordinary blanket, let us say, four skeins of gray and two of white, these she has. All she need do is to wash them to make them ready for use. She will need also two skeins of red. She uses two white skeins for this purpose. She has no black. We might expect her to use two more white skeins but to do so is wasteful and inefficient, for white cannot easily be dyed a pure black. Wool or mohair when given a full dyebath of black are likely to come out gray-blue. They must be dyed several times to make them true black, a necessity prodigal of time and of dye which is costly. She has a large quantity of odds and ends, some black, some indefinite and mixed gray, red and brown leftovers, doubtful white, and even some uncarded lumpy greens and yellows. She has been experimenting in her dyeing for her sandpaintings, dyeing the wool even before carding, and much of it does not satisfy her. All this miscellany she puts away for "black".

She now cards it all, lays aside her feeling for color and gets a variegated lot of yarn. When she has two skeins of this she is prepared to go to the well to give the yarn the final cleansing. She will choose a day when her husband, Curley's-Son, is driving the wagon to fill the water barrels. Her daughter, Ninaba, will go with her. Curley's-Son will water the sheep while she attends to her yarn, and Ninaba, in her scarlet shirt, will dart here and there helping them both.

Since she needs two colors Atlnaba will set two buckets full of water on the brisk fire she makes near the well. While she waits for it to boil she washes the gray and the white skeins in cold water. One soapy wash water and one cold rinse and they are ready to hang up to dry. In the "good old days", that is, before they had soap, the Navajo washed the yarn in yucca suds than which there is no more efficient cleanser. But yucca root, like many other vegetable products, is now much too scarce for that, so ordinary laundry soap is used. In the warm Southwest sun and ever-present wind the white and gray will be nearly dry by the time the other skeins are dyed.

The dyeing is almost as simple as the washing. Those skeins which are dyed are not washed. Atlnaba shakes the dye into the boiling water, stirs it with a stick, lets it come once more to a boil, then puts her white wool into the red, her mixed wool into the black. She boils them until she judges them to be sufficiently dark, approximately half an hour. My own experience shows that the wool takes the dye easily, the mohair even more evenly and readily, although the Navajo say mohair is "hard to dye". Then she squeezes surplus moisture out of the skeins. By this time Curley's-Son has filled the water barrel, and if he and Ninaba have not finished with the sheep, Atlnaba will help them. Because they are almost through she will lay her skeins in the buckets and take them home to dry. As soon as they have dried she may begin her rug.

I have chosen for example the coloring of yarn for a typical modern medium-sized blanket. My supposition has been a modest one, namely, that an old-fashioned color combination is to be used. Accordingly black must be dyed as always. Even if the yarn were spun from the blackest appearing wool, it would become brown or reddish brown within a few years if not dyed. For many years, including those during which I took my lessons, red was the most common of all the colors used. During this time the Navajo used primarily Diamond Dyes which were cheap and easily procured.

Even the more discriminating buyer considers that rug more truly "Navajo" which has the colors white, black, gray *and* red. He often says, "I like red in my blankets." The red used almost exclusively until very recently was a crimson, which if combined with the more quiet colors: tan, gray, white or black, was effective. However, all colors which dye manufacturers see fit to distribute are used. Yellows and oranges, with some greens and purples predominate. Often they are hard and garish, and they seldom combine well with the red.

It is in the use of color secured by aniline dyes that the Navajo rug loses its artistic value. The white tourist is the ultimate consumer. His standards are lax and he knows nothing about Navajo rugs. He sees them hanging from the framework of a roadside shade. They look to him romantic, barbaric. He will take one home for his room. One remark I have often heard made by the more sensitive of his ilk is, "Oh, they are not nearly so nice when you get close to them, are they?"

One reason those he sees are not, is to be laid at the door of his brethren who drive in haste and buy in ignorance. They want something gaudy; they would like it to be large; it must be cheap. Since Navajo rugs are usually sold by weight, large ones, no matter how hideous, are expensive. The jarring color combinations are due more acutely to the buyer's taste than to cheapness. It is true that the Navajo, now that so many things are furnished her, must buy such dyes as are available. If left to herself she would, more often than not, use the more quiet colors, of which she has a good variety. Occasionally she would, as she has in the past, come forth with a daring essay at brilliancy which might turn out to be a stroke of genius.

The history of native handicrafts justifies this assumption. When left to themselves, natives who use colors at all may use brilliant ones, but all natural dyes have a softness rarely secured by our synthetic dyes. Although we have some of the loveliest colors and shades that have ever been achieved in the course of civilization, they are attained by dint of complicated processes, involved chemical and physical formulas which we cannot expect to be successful with the casual methods necessary to the Navajo. These colors are, even in our most sophisticated style centers, rarely seen on cheap articles.

Among the thousands of craftswomen in the tribe there is a generous proportion of real artists. These, I am convinced, would weave if they were never paid a cent for their work. Atlnaba is an example. She spends hours experimenting with the colors at her command. This work is strictly empirical. She may discard a dozen greens and yellows before she accepts one. She may get a satisfactory green today which she will never be able to duplicate if she lives to be a hundred; furthermore, she will not try to.

With all the perfection of modern science and technology, true art remains an intangible dependent upon individual inspiration which has never been defined. It is a combination of factors, some of which are so subtle that they defy analysis. The result of inspiration must so far be laid to chance.

There are, nevertheless, factors which may be controlled; if they are good, the combination of necessary circumstances is more likely to yield pleasing results. The tangible elements which enter into the Navajo rug are materials, craftsmanship and remuneration. The intangibles are the weaver's interest, her experience, and finally, her interpretation of her experience in terms of her materials.

If we grant our artist, not necessarily our mere weaver, the intangibles with that tangible common to even ordinary weavers, virtuosity, and leave for a moment the matter of remuneration, we have left for consideration materials. Those naturally available to our weaver are satisfactory in form and color (see chapters on Wool and Natural Colors). If, however, at one inevitable step in the process, that of dyeing, she is handicapped, it is not likely that the final effect will be laudable even though all other factors are equal.

It is of course true that a real genius can attain even with poor materials. I have seen a few blankets woven from yarn dyed with a mixture of aniline dyes, the resulting shades of which were deep soft browns, warm dark reds and creamy yellows. This is an unusual occurrence because the dyes themselves are complex and recombine in unusual proportions. It is not so rare to find a blanket whose keynote is an unusually soft or delicate shade of the color sought. The green in Atlnaba's sandpainting tapestry is such an example. A yellow combined with a dull dark red—usually I think the worst of color combinations for blankets—used in a mohair web is another. These are exceptions, however, and we are considering the weaver of more ordinary ability.

If she has more acceptable materials the proportion of good blankets will necessarily increase. The proof of this opinion is in such old Navajo blankets as have survived. Many of the early weavers had good materials and the majority of their blankets were good. In primitive society where colors are native and natural and where the striving for aesthetic effects is unaffected, the number of good results is out of all proportion to the number made. Introduce our colors and our methods without the accompanying complicated technique or with no understanding of it and the expectation of real art must be greatly lessened, even abandoned.

For half a century the color in the rugs was left to the Navajo and the manufacturers of dyes.

Since 1931 there have been several movements which aimed to improve the colors of the Navajo blankets. These efforts are based on the supposition that old blankets are the best and that the modern ones should be a throwback to the ancient types. Many of the traders are doubtful as to the value of the movement on the grounds that it is artificial and that at the present time the market for the old-type blanket is small, for it is known primarily as a museum specimen. The Navajo weavers have come so far from this type that almost as much education is required to make it popular with them as for a new article.

The first of these efforts was the attempt to introduce what are called Dupont dyes. These are beautiful in shade and tint and so simple that no end of subtle combinations may be made for other than the primary colors. The Indian women I know like them as a finished product but not enough to use them. The reason is that it requires great care and a long period of time to follow the intricate instructions. Life in a Navajo camp does not warrant fine chemical adjustments. Furthermore, these dyes are initially expensive although they are so potent that a small amount lasts almost indefinitely. Last but not least, they require acetic acid, a harmful product, as a mordant. Anyone who is familiar with the interior of a Navajo hogan knows well that there is no corner or crevice sacred from the prying eyes and hands of the children. This in itself is an overwhelming reason against an enthusiastic adoption of these colors. In two years the attempt to get the Navajo to use these dyes died a natural death which had little to do with the Navajo themselves but rather with the manufacturers of dyes who were restricted by litigation or patent rights.

Wells and Richardson, the makers of Diamond Dyes, who have been selling dyes to the Navajo for many years, then compromised by putting out a series of colors called "Old Navajo Dyes" which are said to be matched to the colors in the old blankets. They are used almost exactly as the regular Diamond dyes and the colors are excellent. I have experimented with them from time to time. The Navajo women like them and of course can use them as well as the others. They have now been used for nearly two years and there is a marked improvement in the blankets I have seen made with them. The original color list supplied bright and dull red, antique scarlet, and dark red, a soft dull yellow and one called canary, a blue which has many possibilities for variation, a dark green which when less intense is soft in effect, orange, a very dark brown, and black.

To these they added in 1934 a rust which is dull reddish brown, a close match to the color I have described in Natural Dyes, Red 12 (p. 42); a tan which is calculated to match the "sand" color of Natural Dyes, Brown 9 (p. 41) and a light green.

These "Old Navajo Dyes" are initially slightly more expensive than the ordinary Diamond Dyes so long in use, but two factors offset this drawback. The Navajo have learned by experience that the same amount as formerly used will dye more wool to a given intensity, and some of the traders who are interested in the improvement of their rugs sell them for the old price and "take their loss", which means really "take a smaller profit".

The Diamond Dyes could be combined in various ways, but the results of combination were usually muddy, and the effects of using diluted dyes as hard as the heavy colors. The improvements of the "Old Navajo Dyes" are beyond estimation, for combinations and shades are usually soft and nearer to "natural" colors. The "hard" ones on the color card are "canary" and "orange" but Navajo wool I have seen dyed with them is usually quite satisfactory. This whole development seems to me to be a step in the right direction.

I have tried the simple device of dyeing carded gray instead of white yarn with pleasing results. The lighter colors are more interesting since the gray is darker to begin with. My favorite color is gray dyed with dull yellow. The result is indescribable, a yarn with a subtle greenish shade. The Navajo women appeared to like my samples. Not enough time has elapsed to show whether or not my friends will take up the idea.

Two major improvements can be made which will vastly improve the quality of the blanket. Such progress is dependent however upon the most fundamental basis of Navajo life, the water supply. Except for the white and gray, Navajo yarn is not washed before dyeing and rarely is it rinsed after the dye-bath. The impurities in the wool must necessarily make the colors dull and cloudy. I made my own experiments where there was plenty of water. I therefore rinsed my yarn two or three times. The first rinse naturally contained a great deal of color, each succeeding one less and less, so that the third had practically none. Although the Diamond dyes are said to be fast one can easily understand that if the yarn is not rinsed after dyeing the dark superfluity of my first rinse must wash out as "run" into the white and gray when the rug undergoes its first bath in the hands of its user.

If each weaver washed her colored yarn in yucca (soapweed) suds, as does her sister who uses vegetable dyes, this difficulty would be overcome. The Navajo woman is not unmindful of this necessity but she is handicapped by circumstances. The truth is, not that she does not want to *use* water, but rather that she does not *have* it to use.

Hastin Gani's Wife was dyeing yarn for a sandpainting blanket fourteen feet by fourteen. It was to have a red background and I watched her, with her simple facilities, dye thirty-six double skeins of white wool red. She is too good a workman to leave her yarn unrinsed but most of the time she was rinsing it in water only a shade paler than the dye-bath itself. At that it took two barrels of water hauled for several miles by wagon before her task was finished. I learned afterward that she had to do it all over again because the skeins of the first batch did not match! This incident is by way of explanation as to why perhaps the Navajo do not do quite as we do. I should add that it occurred during a so-called "dry season". It had not rained for two summers and although there had been plenty of snow in the winter it had evaporated or melted so as to leave no surplus overflow. Seasons like this are not rare in the experience of our desert weavers.

It is not difficult to introduce new ideas to the Navajo women. There are, however, certain necessities fundamental to the success of such a procedure. The idea must be one which is practicable in the environment. Furthermore, it should be thoroughly worked out in all its details and in the utmost simplicity before it is shown to her. The method of teaching is also of greatest importance. It should come about in a natural matter-of-fact way. A woman is not interested in dyeing when she is herding sheep or attending a feast. She cards, spins and dyes when her household tasks are serenely accomplished and there is a lull in her social obligations.

A white woman who is willing to learn what the Navajo woman has to teach her will be the greatest success as a demonstrator. The Indian has much to "show"; she will be glad to "show" her friend. After she has been "shown", the white demonstrator will feel the need of reconsidering her own purpose. If then she finds she has anything left to teach this woman of quiet poise she will know how to teach it and the task will be pleasant and easy.

There is one matter about which the trader should remain firm in encouraging his weavers. He must guard against mis-matching. Carelessness is the only excuse which can be given for using "sheep gray" and "carded gray" in the same design, unless of course as in Atlnaba's case, they have been matched. A particular rug is an unfortunate example. It is large, perhaps four by six feet, the weaving is beyond criticism and the design, which is a combination of Shriner's symbols, is well placed and spaced on a dark gray background. The rug has a black border. It is not a beautiful piece, but more than one Shriner would like it enough to pay the rather large sum it costs. However, there is a portion of the background, a short distance from the center which looks as though grease had been spilled on it. It is the first thing one notices in looking at the blanket and it causes immediate condemnation. The reason for it is that the carder did not match her gray and a goodly portion of it became much darker than the rest. She told the trader that she did not notice it until she had the entire space woven. I can easily believe it because closeness to the loom makes one lose perspective. Nevertheless, she should have ravelled it after she did see it. The work would have been tedious but nothing compared with its present finished uselessness, and the woman's disappointment at the lower price she received for it.

Many blankets have the same fault which, in these days when materials are plentiful can, and should, be overcome (see Pl. XIV, d). Traders who, when all is said and done, have more influence than anyone in preserving and developing the style and standards of the Navajo blankets, are for the most part, critical of mis-matching and do not pay as much for a rug having it. They should continue their custom insisting ever on greater perfection.

There is, on the other hand, danger of overdoing the matter although I do not think it is yet imminent. If the insistence on matching were carried too far, some of the best effects might be missed. The largest element of beauty in the background tan of Atlnaba's sandpaintings is the subtle irregularity of it. It varies from darkish tan to tannish white. I have a bedcover whose background is the lovely rose-tan or sand of the vegetable dye, the most exquisite color the Navajo achieve. There are many shades of it indeed, but the effect is perfect. The design is carried out in black, white and vegetable yellow. For the edge bindings on one side the weaver used a strand of sand and one of vegetable yellow and for the pair on the opposite side one of sand and one composed of a twist of white and one of gray mohair to form its double-ply strand. The effect of such slight irregularities is subtle and better far than exactness. Such inspirations should not be checked.

Perhaps then the emphasis should be laid not so much on matching primarily but rather on the way a wide expanse of self-color is woven. If the darker or lighter shade be carried over a wide part of the web it will blend with the other shades with which it is mingled, but if, as so often happens, the weaver carries her weft only through a narrow part of her warp and finishes several inches, then comes back and fills in the remainder, the rug is almost certain to have the spotted appearance. And what is more, it may not be noticeable until the whole background has been finished.

I have roundly criticised the dyes which the Navajo must use and I think with justification. There is, however, strong hope for at least some of the rugs of the present day based on what has happened to those which are aged in. A great many old rugs are beautiful just because they *are* old. A few persons agree with me that some of the most attractive old pieces were doubtless hideous when they were made. This statement has no reference to those made of bayeta and indigo-dyed yarns, but many blankets were made, even in the old days of more inferior materials. Especially were there colors, then as now, which were anything but fast. There are two things which may happen to dyes. They may fade and when they do usually become soft and beautiful, especially if they fade evenly.

There has always been a tradition that Navajo rugs wash well. In fact washing in suds is the recognized way of cleaning them. Truth is however that not only do they fade but what is worse—and better!—they run. An old blanket which I have coveted for some time has almost every conceivable shade of pink and rose in perfect combination. I do not believe for a moment that one pink strand was woven into it. It was originally red, perhaps even a garish red, white and gray. It was not a red that merely faded but one that ran. In the course of years the fading and running reached their limit and left colors the most expert dyer could not achieve. I have two rugs in my possession which are going through this change. The stage is such an early one that it is not to be admired. It seems to me that the same process is in action, time only will tell whether it will become completely successful.

There is in the blanket collecting avocation the same exaggeration one finds in every similar vogue. Age is of itself a virtue in the minds of those who have lost their perspective, and because a rug is old they refuse to see its faults. The Navajo have a strong veneration for old things. They are fond of old tools, old jewels, old silver, even worn-in garments. They appreciate and admire the beauty of well-made old blankets, but at the same time they see the faults of those which are ill-matched, poorly designed or badly executed. I must needs blush did I feel any responsibility for the remarks my family made about the treasure of a famous collector. And they were right, the color was bad, there was no designing, it was a hit or miss arrangement, and there was no control of the technique.

I think it not impossible that the saddleblanket now used as the floor covering of Old-Mexican's-Son's automobile, or the vegetable dye blanket he uses instead of a tarpaulin when he camps may some day be choice museum exhibits. It is even likely my ordinary rugs, now having a pink instead of a white background, may hang beside them, or that there may be someone who will say they should!

V Natural Colors

Vegetable dyes, fixed with the aid of mineral products, represent a Navajo resource which has not entirely lapsed since the earliest days when they were first adopted. The last ten years, however, have seen a revival of work in vegetable dyes and, I am convinced, experimental additions to ancient practices. Most of the natural colors are good, but I have seen combinations of them which are as ugly as the aniline compositions. They are, however, never gaudy or cheap-looking. The movement for revival has been artistically, and to some extent economically, successful. The majority of the blankets are good in design and color; the small portion of the American public which knows them is willing to pay more for them than for the aniline-dyed ones, thus enabling the traders to pay the Navajo women higher prices.

There is, however, a grave practical drawback. The natural products, vegetable and mineral, are available in quantities too small to be at all adequate for the demands of the numerous good weavers. Some plants which furnish the lovely rose colors have become extinct in parts of the Reservation where they used to grow, because of overgrazing. In those localities where the plants still exist they are becoming scarcer and scarcer. Besides, the process involved in brewing these dyes, though in principle simple enough, is nevertheless so tedious that the average Navajo weaver has no patience for it. There is, therefore, a definite limit to the expansion of this interesting field of color.

Rare pleasure and many surprises are in store for one who has the opportunity of trying the natural dyes. If I were a Navajo woman, I think I should make my blankets of the store dyes as most of them do. But on the days when my imagination soared I should try the various brews generally known but rarely tried; and on the days when my ambition was at its peak I should try out all the plants in my territory adding this and that as occasion should suggest. Just as weaving suggests new patterns so dyeing suggests new formulas.

The rule for making the dyes is quite general. If the part of the plant used is hard, it should be pounded or ground so as to break up the fibers. If it is soft, like petals, bruising is not necessary. The vegetable product thus prepared is boiled in a non-metallic vessel for a longer or shorter time depending on the amount of coloring material, the amount of wool to be dyed, and the shade desired. The concoction is then strained, and the clear liquid boiled with "rock-salt", a mineral which contains aluminum. There are several ways to prepare "rock-salt". Many women heat it in a frying-pan to just the proper consistency. They call it "melting". The melting point is very high. Red Point prefers to "burn" it on hot coals. Naturally it takes skill and care to transfer it from the coals to the dye-bath at exactly the right moment. If one has no "rock-salt", salt and baking soda may be used as a substitute.

After about fifteen minutes the clean dampened wool is immersed in the dye-bath, as always in dyeing, so that it is uniformly wet. The skein of yarn is boiled until the desired shade is attained and is allowed to cool immersed in the dye-bath. When cold, it is washed in suds of the soapweed, thoroughly rinsed and dried.

There are variations on this procedure. Some plants do not require a mordant; some must not be boiled very long; wool should sometimes be dried without rinsing so as to allow for oxidation. I shall indicate the exceptions to the rule with the particular formulas.

Of all the colors extant, the easiest to achieve is yellow. Almost any plant with yellow flowers will yield it, and many will furnish it from a brew of leaves, stems, or both. The yellow is, in almost every case, far better than that of any aniline dye I know. It is with one exception soft and delicate, although the shade depends upon the amount of vegetable product used, the amount of water, and the length of time it is boiled.

I make no pretense of exhausting the possibilities for native dyes. I am recording all I know about them, new ones will continue to be added to our knowledge because of the revival of interest in this subject and because of increasing experimentation.

Yellow

Yellow 1. The foremost of the yellows is that made from the dock or sorrel. The root of this plant consists of many tubers closely resembling sweet potatoes. Each plant furnishes a large amount of the dye-substance so that once the habitat is found an adequate quantity is quickly and easily secured.

The fresh root may be pounded and boiled, or it may be dried and stored indefinitely. The dried root should be ground. Several handfuls of the fresh root boiled in about ten quarts of water yields a lemon yellow, a clear definite color, the hardest of any I tried out.

If more of the root is used and it is boiled longer, the result is a dark, soft orange or orange-brown, an entirely satisfactory color. An infinite number of gradations may be secured by varying the conditions.

Since this is one of the best-known tannin-producing plants (Canaigre), it needs no mordant. Some Navajo are empirically aware of the tannin content and do not use the "rock-salt"; others, following the usual rule of thumb, use it. For the same reason also, the iron of a metallic vessel reacts to form a red-brown or mahogany color (see p. 42).

The Franciscan Fathers[1] describe a process by which old gold is obtained by crushing the fleshy root of the dock with "rock-salt" on a metate and rubbing the resulting paste into the wool. The Hopi use this process without the mordant, but add a little water to it and soak

[1] An Ethnologic Dictionary of the Navaho Language, p. 231.

basket reeds in it to obtain a lemon yellow. At first sight it seems a Hopi technique, but the man who told me about it added that a Hopi living at Leupp had married a Navajo woman who showed the informant's family how to use this plant.

Yellow 2. A beautiful, soft yellow may be secured by treating the flowers of one of the goldenrods (Bigelovia)[1] exactly as I outlined for the most general rule. At Black Mountain it is made without a mordant.

A weaver told me that if one uses only the stems and leaves of this plant in large quantity and boils the concoction a long time, "all day", a dark green will result. I did this, but obtained a dark, pleasing yellow. I tried my experiment late in August, and I believe her instructions might result as she predicted if the plant were taken earlier in the season, when it is more succulent.[2]

Another explanation may be that green to my Navajo friend is not green to me. In my experience all the colors which the Navajo call green, except those made of indigo, are more yellow, verging only slightly toward green. However, the color I obtained by this method did not even "verge"!

Yellow 3. The "owl's-claw" is a plant which would be more useful if it were not such a pest. It is sometimes called "South American rubberweed" or "sneezeweed", and it finds itself much at home in the Navajo desert. It is poisonous to sheep and goats. It rapidly supplants useful vegetation in the regions where it becomes established. No amount of digging will discourage it. Digging it out seems to have the effect of cultivating it. The Navajo name it from the root, which has the shape of an owl's foot. The rootlets are incredibly tenacious, the most hair-like having the ability to survive. Rain,

[1] I suspect those of any of the native goldenrods will do.
[2] The reader can readily understand my pleasure, after having written this sentence, to find in Amsden "....if the dyer is careful to include only the mature blossoms of the shrub, a clear yellow will result, but if immature flowers, leaves or green bark are used, a green tint....will appear". (Navaho Weaving, p. 85.)

which is scarce, is the only thing which kills it. It has one use, however, for its flowers treated according to the general rule make a splendid soft yellow dye.

Yellow 4. A yellow much like that of yellow 3 (in fact, I can hardly tell the difference without consulting my labels) I secured from treating the leaves of sage according to the general rule. Where we live this is easy to procure, and it is the simplest of the dyes to concoct.

Yellow 5. A yellow can be made from mistletoe, a parasite on juniper. This is a bright, clear, almost lemon yellow.

Brown

Under "brown" I am including, besides the real brown, some colors difficult to describe and impossible to reproduce by printing processes. They include the "sand" color or pinkish tan, which is, in my opinion, the best color the Navajo make. The regular browns vary, of course, from light tan to dark, rich browns; some are nearer to yellow, others approach red. Some are muddy, others are clear, depending upon the plant used, its concentration and the time of boiling. They, like the yellows, may be obtained from many products.

Brown 6. (a) A clear, dark, rich brown is obtained from boiling the shells of walnuts. Since no mordant is used in this dye, it is likely that the Navajo are aware of the tannic acid content. (b) A lighter brown but different from (a), not just a shade, is made from the young twigs of the walnut.

Brown 7. The brown secured from this formula is really a tan. We pounded about a quart of the leaves and stems of the cliffrose and added to them about two handfuls of pounded juniper branches. We followed the usual procedure and secured two colors. That secured by boiling the mixture in an enamel kettle was a clear tan, but toward yellow. The wool dyed in the aluminum bucket has the pinkish cast I so admire. Presumably the tannic acid of the juniper caused hydrolysis of the aluminum salt to form a lake. It is even possible that the cliffrose contains tannin. I have never had the opportunity to try these plants separately.

Brown 8. From the stems of the plant called "Navajo tea" the pinkish tan may be obtained. The plant is not plentiful everywhere. The Hastin Gani's always have a good supply. We drank it at their place and also at the home of their daughter. It is thought to be good for indigestion. It has a pleasantly mild, aromatic taste. The Navajo always add a great deal of sugar to the brew, which makes it sickeningly sweet, somewhat like licorice water.

The process for making this dye is probably the general one. We never had enough of this plant to try the dye.

Brown 9. The color made by this formula is, in my opinion, the best which the Navajo make. It is neither brown, tan, nor red, but has elements of all three. Although a neutral color, it is lively and is much like the pink of the sandstone cliffs in the light of late afternoon.

It is made by boiling the bark of the root of mountain mahogany, adding a small quantity of juniper or spruce branches, and fixing with "rock-salt". The dyeing is easy. The preparation of a sufficient quantity of the root is at best a back-breaking job. The shrub is not plentiful; when found, the roots must be dug out with a grubbing hoe, and later pounded thoroughly. It is possible to use the entire root but only the bark contains color, and a satisfactory quantity of the root is likely to be too bulky for an ordinary vessel used in dyeing. It took us a whole day to collect the amount we used, another day to grind the bark and dye the yarn. When we had finished, we had enough for two large skeins of the lightest shade. I had always admired this color of the Navajo dyes, but after this experience a large blanket with background of this color, well matched, seems to me superior in craftsmanship and effort to all the other blankets the Navajo make.

Red 10. A variation on the theme of the mountain mahogany, and that a complicated one, makes the brightest of the native colors. To the dye-bath obtained by boiling the roots of the mountain mahogany, ashes obtained from burning juniper twigs and the powdered bark of black alder are added, and to this mixture some of the ground lichen. The color will depend upon the proportion of the ingredients, but the amount of juniper ash and of lichen is relatively small as compared with the quantity of mountain mahogany root bark and of alder. It will vary from soft pink to a dark magenta, passing through many brilliant shades of rose. The brightness and richness of the colors obtained in this process depend upon boiling and concentration. One woman who had brought in a blanket containing red which was exactly like aniline dye said she had boiled the yarn five times, allowing it to dry after each bath.

Red 11. The fruit of the prickly pear is the source of cardinal which cannot be differentiated from that of commercial dyes. To about two quarts of the fruit which must be dead ripe, about a cupful of "rock-salt" and a handful of the bark or roots of Colorado blue spruce are added, and the whole is steeped in about two gallons or more of water.

Red 12. I think it best to include the dark, rich mahogany color we obtained from dock under "red". It could be classed as accurately under "brown". We used dock root as I described for Yellow 1. But we boiled it in an aluminum pail, and when we added salt and soda the deep orange solution became bright red. The wool after boiling and rinsing was a most desirable, dark, brownish red. It is likely that the tannic acid of the dock root causes the same change with aluminum as that described for Brown 7.

Red 13. I have heard of another red which a woman near Ganado made by mixing several products she used for other colors. I was not able to get the names of the items.

Red 14. The same material which furnishes the red for the sand-paintings (red ochre) is the basis of one of the brilliant rose dyes. I was not able to learn any more about this.

Blue and Green

Blue 15. The deep tones of blue and its derivatives are to a great extent made of indigo. In the early days indigo was secured by the Indians of the Southwest from Mexico; since trade with the Whites has been lively, it is all obtained from them. Dyeing with indigo was a simple but long drawn-out process. The necessary amount of indigo was dissolved in urine, the yarn was immersed in it and allowed to soak for a long period; fifteen days was long enough for a dark navy. When the proper shade had been obtained, the wool was rinsed, "*often*," said Red Point, "sometimes as many as fifteen times."

Urine was collected in special pots kept in the house for the purpose. Only that of young children was used. The Navajo believed that if the urine of persons no longer virgin were used the dye would streak the wool, and the color would not be fast.

At the present time wool is still dyed blue by the same process, but the pressure of white prudery has made it a secret. Several old women, on being consulted, evaded the answer, "But", volunteered each hopefully, "if you give me the yarn I will dye it blue (or green) for you". Then I, being not unwilling to mention "the word" asked bluntly, "Do you use urine?" Whereupon the informant, surprised at my knowledge but pleased that there was no longer need for dissimulation, advanced in every case the same information.[1]

Although the process of dyeing with indigo is simple, its success is based upon somewhat complicated chemical facts. Indigo, which is insoluble in water, is reduced by fermentation caused by micro-

[1] Amsden's discussion (p. 88) corroborates my results.

örganisms and the ammonia furnishes the necessary alkaline solution. The result of the reduction is called "indigo white", a substance soluble in water, which enters the wool and turns to a blue when exposed to the air. The blue is a result of oxidation and, being insoluble in water, is a fast color.

I have previously noted the fact that all greens I have seen done with Navajo vegetable products are more yellow than green. I have, however, a few formulas I have not tried myself which are said to make green. True green is a combination of indigo combined with yellow. Indigo should not be excluded from the vegetable dyes. The only objection to it is the fact that it is not native, but has always been secured by trade.

Blue 16. It is said that a blue dye is secured from the petals of the larkspur. Since this grows in restricted localities and since the amount of blue the petals contain is small, it must be a tremendous task to secure enough to dye even a small amount of yarn. I have never been in the Navajo country in the season when larkspur blooms, so have not seen dye made of the petals. They should be boiled only fifteen minutes or less. "Rock-salt" is used for the mordant. (Mrs. Nanaba Bryan, instructor of Navajo weaving, has made all kinds of experiments with native products. She tells me she has had no success with this formula). Any blue flower may be used in the same way; nowadays, alfalfa is a favorite.

Blue 17. Long ago the Navajo traded a mineral, "one of the molybdenum compounds closely allied to ilsemamnite. It has never been reported from the molybdenum deposits at Questa, New Mexico, but might possibly have occurred there in the past. There is an apparently rather large deposit of it near Ouray, in northeastern Utah, which may possibly have been the source of these dyes". This quotation is from a report made by Mr. Edwin Eckel of the U. S. Geological Survey, for Mr. Lorenzo Hubbell. He adds that the black sandstones there yield a blue solution which is a good dye for silk, poor for cotton. Mr.

Eckel has no information on wool, but since the dye is good for silk, also an animal fiber, it is doubtless satisfactory for wool as well. He adds that dye manufacturers previously used a molybdenum compound which has been supplanted by synthetic indigo. The ancient process used by the Navajo was perhaps the same as that used with indigo. It is possible that they traded with the Indians living between them and Ouray. The distance is not so great, nor is the trading so indirect as from Mexican sources.[1]

Given a dependable source of blue, the derivatives are not difficult to make.

Green 18. Of all the many yellows, dock is the richest in color and supply, and the simplest to use. Yarn is dyed green by first putting it through the indigo bath of Blue 1. Then the blue yarn is dyed "yellow" exactly as I have described it for Yellow 1. The result is green.

Green 19. A yellow-green commonly seen is made by brewing the leaves and stems of one of the goldenrods (Bigelovia) called by some Whites "tall rattlesnake weed", by others "sneezeweed" (see Yellow 2).

Purple

The weavers in the vicinity of Black Mountain have developed a new style of native-dye blanket which consists of combinations of dull gold, rose, and dark purple. Black and the gray-blue, an incomplete color, secured by dyeing white yarn black, may also be used. The result is good indeed, but with only ordinary knowledge of Navajo blankets, a person might well consider them as non-Navajo. The purple is deep, dark, and soft. I suppose it is made by combining indigo and red.

[1] It is possible that the blue of the "patchwork cloak" described by Wyman and Amsden (The Masterkey. Vol. VIII [1934]: 136) was from the molybdenum compound.

Purple 20. The petals of the four-o' clock are boiled for fifteen minutes or less, and "rock-salt" is used as a mordant. A large amount of the coloring material is needed and it should be boiled for only a short time.

Black

Black. Of all the dyes used by the Navajo, black is the most trying to make. It is really a tannin ink, the chief ingredient of which, lampblack, must be made by the natives. The tannin-yielding body is secured by boiling twigs, leaves and berries of the aromatic sumac for a long time. The second requirement is an iron salt. For this the Navajo use yellow ochre, which they burn until a different iron oxide is formed (red ochre). Finally, a mucilaginous agent is necessary to keep the insoluble matter in suspension. Gum from the pine or piñon furnishes this element.

Skill is required to heat the combination of powdered ochre and gum, which is highly inflammable, sufficiently to allow carbonization to take place without igniting the mixture. By the exertion of the proper skill and sufficient patience the sticky mass becomes gradually drier, until lampblack is formed. The iron salt, combined with the tannins obtained by boiling the sumac, makes a satisfactory ink which "takes" well on wool. It is intensified by the lampblack which remains finely suspended in the solution, acting as a sort of filler to give body to the mixture. The resulting substance is intense and fast.

Red Point was well aware of the fact that his daughters and I had no knowledge of the technique of heating the ingredients properly, and no knowledge of the principles involved. He told us that a menstruating woman should never expect to have success at making this black dye. It would not be fast. He derives his own experience from burning plants for medicinal purposes. Illness and the need for "sings" interfered with his plan of showing us the process.

[46]

In contrast to the dyes the weavers sometimes use a whitener. Ordinarily the natural color of wool, a soft creamy white, is considered satisfactory. Occasionally a pure dead white is desirable, as, for example, in making contrasts in sandpainting blankets. The white wool is rinsed after washing in water to which a white clay, finely ground, has been added. When used in this way, it acts as a filler, and falls out of the woven yarn as fine dust. This substance is called montmorillonite and is highly adsorptive.[1]

The materials and processes discussed in this chapter and the resulting knowledge doubtless represent an old fund of primitive attainment. Many of the weavers are empirically aware of the chemical changes which take place. Certain of the dyestuffs contain tannin and the observant weavers use no mordant with them. The more ordinary, unamenable to the results of experiment, proceed by rule of thumb and add the mordant even when it is unnecessary, thereby causing no harm, but adding nothing to the tribal knowledge.

It is to be noted as a matter typically Navajo that in all the formulas I have given I have not referred to the exact amount of the items used, but have said rather "a little", "about", "a handful". Never is anything measured exactly, but the weaver uses her judgment or accedes to her circumstances. The reason for this is the casual life the Navajo leads, taking advantage of the means at his disposal—all of which are of necessity variable and uncertain. One day the weaver has much water, next week she has not even enough for cooking purposes. She may wish to use a dye which requires a whole day's boiling and have everything she needs but wood. She may have much yarn and little dyestuff, or much dye and little yarn. She may lack only the handful of lichen or Colorado spruce she needs.

In some cases she puts off the work until she has everything she needs, but more frequently she uses makeshifts. If she has no Colorado blue spruce, she uses juniper; lacking dock for yellow, she resorts

[1] Personal information from Mr. Edwin Eckel.

to sage or "owl's claw". Wishing to make a design which requires an equal amount of dye for two colors, she has an abundance of only one, a little of the other. She therefore changes the design she had in mind. Sometimes she is not satisfied with the new solution of her problem, sometimes she likes it better than her original idea, and often she has learned much. Variety, subtlety, originality and inimitability are frequent and pleasing results of her conditions and the resourcefulness with which she meets them.

VI Implements

Just as the cook takes for granted her need of pots, pans, and kettles, so the weaver casually supplies herself with the implements of her craft. They are simple enough, made of "hard wood", but nevertheless indispensable. I have already noted the need for a pair of towcards for carding; these must be secured from the trader since the Navajo have no way of making them. The spindle has also been mentioned as a necessity. It consists of a stick, slightly tapered at the end, near the butt end of which a whorl of wood or stone is fastened.

A set of battens or broad sticks is needed. When the weaver begins to weave she uses a batten perhaps three inches wide (Pl. V, *a*) to run through the shed made by separating alternate warps. For about the first quarter of the weaving, if the rug is two or more feet long, the warps are loose and it is easy to insert the wide batten. The wider it is, the more space the fingers have through which to carry the weft. As the weaving progresses, the warp becomes tighter and tighter and the use of a narrower batten facilitates the throwing of the sheds. When the weaver is within a few inches of the top she will be using the narrowest stick in her set, a reed not more than a quarter of an inch wide which has been flattened at one end. She has, therefore, a whole set of battens which vary from three inches wide and two and one-half feet long, to only one-quarter inch in width and about nine inches in length.

The batten is broader at the top than at the bottom, its ends being slightly cut away at one side. It has a slight bend which shape makes it easier to pick up the individual warps. The curve of the batten is secured partially by shaping when the wood is green and partially by subsequent use.

Weavers of other tribes, especially if they use a shuttle so that the design extends across the entire width of the blanket, use the batten to drive home the weft. It is inserted into the shed vertically, turned to horizontal in which position it remains while the weft is inserted, then turned to vertical again and pressed down with considerable force. Some Navajo weavers, making a stripe or self-design, do this too; but none depends upon it exclusively for making her fabric tight, and it would not be adequate for that weaving which covers only a part of the warp. The women of Red Point's family never use the batten at all to pound the weft because it weakens the warp. They depend entirely on the use of the comb for this purpose.

Every weaver has a set of combs varying in size. Red Point's women prefer broad, heavy, short ones for ordinary use, but they have all sizes. The weight of Maria Antonia's favorite comb recompenses her for not using the batten for pounding. A slim slight comb with only a few long teeth is just right for combing weft where it fits into an angle already formed. Very small ones serve for pushing, rather than pounding, when the weaving is within two inches of the end. There is no space through which to pound and the comb pushes weft up and down between the warps. One large and one small comb are enough for ordinary purposes. Most weavers have at least four and many have more.

Although the weft of Navajo blankets is most frequently manipulated by the fingers, the simplest mechanical device aids them when weaving a large expanse of self-color. It is merely a reed about an eighth of an inch in diameter with broken ends. The weaver catches the yarn over the roughness of the end of the reed, then winds it diagonally from end to end of the reed, taking care not to wind too much yarn on it, for that makes it bulge in the middle, and it will catch on the warps as it is pushed through the shed. This crude reed is the only approach to a shuttle in the Navajo weaver's kit. Three or four of them will do; most weavers have a large supply which they gather for themselves if the reeds grow in their vicinity, or trade from those women who can secure them easily.

No batten is small enough to use at the very end of the weaving, when only half an inch remains to be filled in. The weft may then be carried by a sacking-needle. If the weaver has only one, it should be a fine one or at least not more than medium-sized. Maria Antonia used the end of an umbrella rib with an eye in it for the same purpose. Its end is flat like that of the narrow batten, and, since it is flatter than the sacking-needle, it is more efficient.

Just as every needle-woman prefers a particular thimble or pair of scissors, so every weaver has her favorite batten and comb. New implements are not very good; they are rough and thick. The Navajo weaver insists that battens and combs be made of wood which is hard, tough, and easily polished. The reason those of an experienced weaver look admirably smooth and dark in color, like old furniture long used, is that they have been worn by repeated journeys through the woolen warp which is a perfect polisher. Besides, the weaver has trimmed them to her comfort. A new comb, occasionally even a very old one, may splinter or split. The weaver takes out her knife (more frequently a paring- than a pen-knife) and shaves it off until it is again suitable. She will whittle down the pointed end also, if it is too blunt for her purposes.

The Navajo weaver, like any highly skilled workman, can mend her tools; if occasion demands, she can even make them. If, however, she has a husband, a brother, or a father, she is not likely to do so. Even as she shows her pride in her menfolk by weaving them choice saddleblankets, so they express their affection and interest in her work by fashioning her tools and setting up her loom.

One of the battens we used at Red Point's must have been at least forty years old. It belonged to Maria Antonia, and her daughters had the same fondness for it that I had. It had tradition behind it; by its smoothness and the perfect adaptation of its form it enkindled a lively emotion of respect in her who was allowed to use it or even to handle it. The end of the spindle used by Left-Handed Singer was worn flat on one side so as to fit exactly into the shape of his thumb where it rested. Maria Antonia used on her favorite spindle a whorl of sandstone which one of her grandsons had picked up near a ruin. It was old, smooth and unique. All the women were proud of it. One day Yikadezba, with the genius of a two-year-old, broke it, and there was universal regret, although destruction on the part of children ordinarily evokes only a tolerant smile and a shrug of the shoulder.

Sometimes old implements can be bought from their owners easily enough. Without coaxing I bought from Juan's wife a comb whose texture is like that of old silver. I doubt if I could have bought Maria Antonia's favorite batten or Left-Handed Singer's spindle.

I came by a complete set of weaving tools quite fortunately. While at Red Point's the first summer I used the tools belonging to my grandmother and sisters. Toward the end of my stay a trader friend offered me a complete kit. Years before, a woman had gone to Albuquerque to serve as an exhibit weaver. She had sent back for her kit; the trader had sent it. It missed its destination—the woman doubtless went by a different name in Albuquerque from the one by which she was known on the Reservation—and it was returned to him. He had it for years, for no Navajo would think of buying such things. He very kindly gave it to me. I have added to it from time to time and the set is quite satisfactory for medium-sized blankets.

PLATE III

[a]
Second spinning

[b]
Spinning warp

[c]
Twisting ply cord

[d]
Simple cat's cradle for triple-ply cord

PLATE IV

[a]
Stringing warp

[b]
Twining at end of warp

[c]
Binding warp to beam

[d]
Adjiba's loom (courtesy J. L. Hubbell Trading Post)

VII Warp Stringing

Unlike the European weaver who has her loom made for her, the Navajo makes hers as she goes. The setting up of the warp involves at the same time the manufacture of the loom. It is literally a device of sticks and strings, in its parts and even in its entirety, the simplest of machines which, in all its simplicity, lacks none of the essentials of that colossus of the weaving industry, the Jacquard loom.

There are three phases of warp stringing, each involving a different part of the loom, all interrelated. The frame upon which the warp is strung is temporary; the sticks to which the warp is fastened after being strung, together with the warp secured to them, constitute the moveable part of the loom; the loomframe is the permanent part of the device to which the moveable parts must be fastened before weaving can be undertaken.

Warpframe

It is of primary importance that the warp be carefully strung. Any mismeasurement, crossing of threads, or irregularity will follow the weaver from the first essential motion until she sets in the last weft thread. It is far better to guard against mistakes than to correct them, for although correction is possible, a mistake, like a ghost, is rarely entirely laid.

Warp is often strung outside the hogan or at a place where there is no loomframe to which the warp stringing has no necessary relation.

The warpframe, like all other parts of the loom, is constructed casually as the woman works. Two long poles form its sides; they should be slightly elevated from the ground. In Pl. IV, *a* Atlnaba laid them on rocks. Maria Antonia, in stringing my first three blankets, used short beams about six inches square in cross-section. The distance between the edge poles need not be nearly as great as the width of the blanket, for the warp is never spread to its full width while on the warpframe.

The crosspieces are laid on top of the side poles and fastened securely. The distance between them is about two inches less than the length of the rug; the two inches allow for the stretching of the warp. The photograph shows that Atlnaba fastened her crosspieces (which are broomsticks) by intertwining strong three-ply cord about them and the edge poles so that they could not slip. However, since her poles had no crotches or convenient protuberances, she drove a strong nail in front of each crosspiece on either side so that it could not move. She then used the nail so that it would keep cord as well as crosspiece from slipping.

When the warpframe, lying horizontally on the ground, is complete and every piece of it has been made rigid, the warp-stringer takes up her position as in Pl. IV, *a* and fastens the end by tying a loop around the upper stick. She then carries the ball back and forth always *over* each stick. As the ball leaves her right hand to fall down and under the stick, her left hand holds the warp firmly at the top of the stick. If the warp is always carried in the same direction, namely *over* the sticks, there will be no confusion and the sheds will be regularly formed at the center. The woman pushes the loops at each end close together, but tries to keep those at one end nearly opposite those at the other.

When she has what she considers enough loops to furnish the width of her blanket, she ties the warp at the end opposite the first loop she made, but does not tear the warp, for the tie is only temporary. She next measures off two lengths of edge cord, which she has carefully selected for color and tightness of twist. She doubles it and ties a loop knot at the folded end leaving the two ends free, as she prepares to make the twined edge of the blanket.

To do this she changes her position. Instead of sitting inside the warpframe (Pl. IV, *a*) she sits outside it at one end (Pl. IV, *b*) and dexterously twines the two loose ends of her end cords so as to form a neat binding (see Lesson 6). This twining determines the space between the warps. If the cord is thick, the warps will stand far apart (perhaps one-quarter to three-eighths of an inch) as they do in the "vegetable dye" blankets. If the binding thread is slender, the space between the warps is small (not more than one-eighth of an inch). The distance between the warps depends not only on the thickness of the binding strands, but also on how tight the weaver pulls them. A good weaver always avoids tightness in any operation. The test of her craftsmanship is to get tension just right. She must take care also not to give the warps too much leeway. This she does by complete coördination of her fingers and the cords and by the exercise of good judgment which comes with practice.

When Marie was stringing my second blanket, I asked her to let me bind one end while she did the other. When we were finished, the warp at my end was half a hand narrower[1] than that at her end. We were then obliged to push the warp, strand by strand, along the binding cords until they were spread evenly over the same width at one end as at the other.

If, when she has bound the required width which she measures off hand by hand, the worker finds that the warp has been carried over the stick too many times, she unwinds the surplus from the warpframe onto her warp ball. If there are not enough loops she supplies the required number. Strangely, it is not often necessary to do much in the way of adding or subtracting. The expert, although she does not count, judges the measurements remarkably well with her eye. When she has wound the last warp loop she needs, she fastens the end by the same kind of knot she used at the diagonally opposite corner when

---

[1] A hand is the distance from the end of the thumb to the end of the middle finger, in other words, a span.

she began the stringing. She finishes off her twining strands by tying them in a loop knot. At this stage the length and the width of the blanket are fixed and sheds for the ordinary weave are made. The worker preserves the sheds by placing a reed on each side of the middle where the crossing of the strands forms them (Fig. 1). She is now finished with the warpframe. She unties the top sticks and withdraws them. She has before her a mass of warp curls which, however, has unity and form. The twining controls the size and position of the

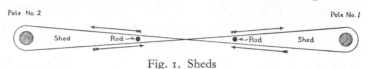

Fig. 1. Sheds

ends, the reeds hold in place the threads which form the respective sheds. The long side poles and the shorter thick ones which support them may now be removed. The warpframe is large and awkward, even when set up for only a small rug.

When Maria Antonia and Marie strung the warp for my second rug, they used as supports for the warpframe the lower crosspiece of the permanent loomframe and only one of their other knotty long poles which they placed parallel with the crosspiece.

If the rug to be strung is to be unusually long, the side poles of the loomframe must be somewhat longer. It is not easy to get poles even fifteen feet long, such as Hastin Gani's Wife needed for her sandpainting blanket, but it is possible. There are many rugs much longer than this. When a blanket longer than a woman's convenient reach in each direction, let us say six feet at the greatest, is to be strung she will have help. Each woman will take up her position within the frame near the crosspole over which the warp is to pass. After one woman has fastened the end she will roll the ball to her helper who will pass it over the pole at her end and roll it back. They will thus continue until the warp is strung.

Although the weaving of large rugs entails complications not present in weaving small ones, there is no difference in the method or the principles involved. The complexities are merely additional ones having to do with the awkwardness of size which, of course, require extra care.

I have worked out no sophisticated substitute for the warpframe. I string my warp in this primitive fashion.

VIII Setting up the Loom

The warp-setter has stretched her warp to the desired length, has strung enough of it to furnish the width, and has bound both ends so that they match. Except for the reeds which separate her sheds all parts of the loomframe which have supported the threads and made them shapely have been removed. She next begins to construct that part of her loom which may be called

The Moveable Loom

She takes one of the smooth and usually, but not necessarily, round sticks, which she has ready. The sticks she uses for this part of her loom may be the same as those used for the crosspieces of her warp-frame. Usually, however, a weaver is more particular about having smoother, more shapely sticks for the loom proper than for the warp-frame.

She lays before her the amorphous-looking, but actually orderly, mass of warp, with the center rods horizontal. She then holds the smooth stick firmly in her left hand and lays one twined end of the warp along it. She ties the end of the warp near the end of the stick by winding some strong, medium-weight string around it. She allows the loopknot to project at the right of the wound string to prevent the warp binding from slipping out of place, and may even cut a groove near the end of the stick so that the binding cord can settle into it firmly. She stretches the binding edge to the width desired for the rug and fastens it in the same way at the opposite end. When she is sure both ends are secure, she winds the string about stick and warp twining, at regular intervals, until she comes to the end where she carefully fastens the binding cord.

[58]

For ordinary sized rugs, up to six feet wide let us say, the cord is carried between every two warp loops, but for the larger ones, the weaver may make the intervals longer. Hastin Gani's Wife wound hers between every three warp loops. Here, as in every other process involved, firmness is the consideration. The warp will remain in place better if it is tightly bound to the beams; it will be more tightly bound if it is wound closely.

Rugs are sometimes seen which have a scalloped instead of a straight edge. The reason for this is that the weaver bound the warp to the beams too loosely, she carried the binding cords through the warp at intervals too wide, so that the warp loops between the binding were pulled out of line by the tightening cord of the loom proper.

The warp is now loosely controlled by the rods at the center and firmly bound by a loomstick at one end. The weaver repeats the operation for the other end. Before binding it tightly to the second loomstick she measures to be sure the width is exactly the same at one end as the other. If it is not, she can easily pull the warp loops in their loosely twined binding closer or space them farther apart. If there is much of a discrepancy, as there was when Marie twined one end and I the other, she divides the difference carefully along the entire width. If the difference is small, as it is if Marie twines both ends herself, it may be taken up by adjusting only two or three warp loops.

At this point the worker is ready to combine the moveable loom with the loomframe, the permanent part of the loom which stands in some convenient spot of every weaver's home.

The Loomframe

The loomframe consists simply of two uprights and two crosspieces of heavy wood (Fig. 2). The Navajo cut the uprights from piñon. Naturally they trim off the branches but they do not smooth down

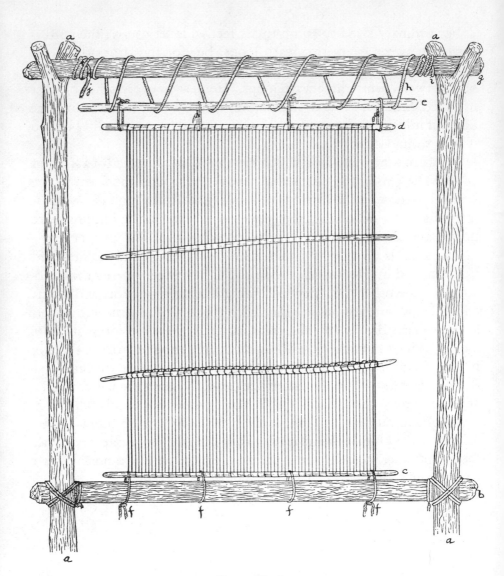

Fig. 2. The loom

too much the portions from which they are cut. They skin off the bark, but somewhat carelessly. They may leave a fork at the top of the two uprights, so that the upper crosspiece may be laid in the crotches. The pieces are cut according to the place where the loomframe is to be set up. The tapering tops of my uprights could easily be fitted between the rafters, since my loom was to be set up in a house with a log roof.

The lower crosspiece must be quite heavy, and fastened firmly below. Mine was made rigid by driving two wedges into the earth floor on opposite sides of it at each end. Sometimes there is an arrangement consisting of a buried stringer to which the lower crosspiece may be securely fastened. It is of prime importance that the two uprights and lower crosspiece of the frame be absolutely rigid.

The uprights, as well as the lower crosspiece, must be firm. The thick upper crosspiece must be moveable so that it can be raised or lowered according to the size of the blanket and of the rope which regulates the warp tension. Its ends rest, however, when adjusted, in a sort of network of balewire or strong cord bound around each of the uprights at the proper level. The network, which is quite shapeless, is so arranged that the more heavily the beam settles with the downward pull exerted by the weight of the beam and the greater the downward strain on it, the firmer it becomes.

Navajo loomframes are not by any means all in houses. Outside, they may be fastened in the earth below and to trees at the top, or other devices may be resorted to. Each household always has one, but very often two or three in various places, both outdoors and in.

We who live in houses and apartments cannot depend upon the earth in which to fasten our looms. I have had a loomframe constructed which is quite satisfactory, at least for such small and medium-sized blankets as I am likely to weave at home. It is the result of a number of suggestions. At the Navajo vocational school at Fort Wingate weaving is taught. The Navajo instructor needed many looms to accommodate large classes and they had to be installed indoors. She designed a loomframe which is much like mine but much larger and so deep that two women can weave at the same time, one on each side of the loom. The difference is only of degree, not of principle.

A loom is bulky and awkward and one may not wish to have it about all the time. A cabinet-maker made one for me with the two uprights fastened to the crosspieces with mortise and tenon. The arrangement left much to be desired, however, in firmness, so we added braces which are fastened with screws. A friend of mine uses dowels which are even more convenient. The upper crosspiece should correspond to the upper crosspiece of the Navajo loom, but with us it is an additional element which holds the frame together. To take the place of the Navajo element, I have used a curtain pole which fits into holes made in the uprights at different levels thus allowing for differences in the length of the blankets. This difference may also be regulated by using a longer or shorter tightening cord within certain limits.

An additional element is the presence of legs or supports placed at right angles to the uprights. They serve to preserve the balance of the loomframe, and take the place of the Navajo buried beam or wedging into the earth. For we must guard against having the loom falling forward when the strong pressure necessary to throwing the sheds is brought to bear upon it. The loomframe may be assembled easily and when I am finished with my weaving I can easily take it down.

Since I am quite comfortable in the Navajo sitting position, I am satisfied to have my frame at floor height. There is no reason why it should not be fastened to a platform so that the weaver who must sit on a chair can weave at ordinary sitting-height. Adjustments of this kind can always be made; no one is freer to make them than the Navajo weaver. So far the most necessary principles are strength and rigidity. If all elements are firmly fastened to allow for great resistance against a downward and forward pull, there will be no trouble.

[62]

The loomframe is always ready for our weaver. She has her warp ready to fasten to the loomframe. The combination of these two parts may now be properly called a "loom", or, "the loom proper".

The Loom Proper

After both ends of the warp are firmly bound to sticks, it is a matter of chance, not of calculation, as to which end becomes the web- and which the warp-beam for up to this point they are the same. The worker fastens lengths of string loosely over a stick considerably longer than the warp width, so that if they are stretched, the stick, Fig. 2, *e*, will lie parallel to the stick, Fig. 2, *d*, holding the warp at a distance of from four to six inches. Each length is about ten to twelve inches from the next, the first being tied near the end but between two warp strands. By tying the extra stick *e* to this end the weaver decrees that it shall be the upper or warp-beam.

The stick *c* which she fastens to the lower beam, *b*, of the loomframe is the web-beam. It is fastened with balewire or strong cord (Fig. 2,*f*) to the lower crosspiece of the loomframe. The number of ties will depend on the width of the blanket. Three are sufficient for a narrow blanket; five or more must be used for a wider one. The web-beam should be tied at intervals of about ten or twelve inches. It is better to have too many than not enough, for these fastenings will have to bear the maximum strain. The warp-beam is usually tied to stick *e* above as many times as the web-beam is bound below and the fastenings are nearly opposite.

One end of wire is carried under the beam of the loomframe from back to front, up and over both the permanent beam and the web-beam, between the warps to the back of the loom. There it meets the other end of the wire, is given several deft twists to make it incapable of giving or slipping, and the ends are turned down so that the materials will not catch into them subsequently. I forgot to list a pair of pliers among the implements. They are convenient but not necessary, for strong cord may be used instead of balewire in every case. The fact is that wire is more commonly used nowadays for most purposes where it is adequate. Most Navajo have pliers.

As soon as the web-beam is firmly in place the weaver adjusts the thick rope (Fig. 2, *h*) to the upper (and moveable) crosspiece of the loomframe. This involves experimentation with the height of the crossbeam (Fig. 2, *g*). It starts at the back and is carried over from back to front and under again toward the back. One end of the rope hangs down for three to eight inches of its length and is made firm merely by being caught under the first wind, as in Fig. 2, *i*. After being wound around the crossbeam several times the rope is carried under the stick (Fig. 2, *e*) near the end. The wrapping is continued over the crossbeams from back forward and under stick *e* from front to back at reasonably short intervals (from four to twelve inches), until the whole stick has been included. The rope is carried about the crossbeam *g* several times more after leaving stick *e* and is casually fastened by allowing the end to drop under the last wind of rope, as in Fig. 2, *j*.

The arrangement of this rope and its even relationship to stick *e* is of the utmost importance because it regulates the warp tension. This arrangement is the most usual and convenient for a right-handed person. With the rope in this position it may be tightened easily by pressing on the back parts of it with the right hand and taking up the slack with the left, holding it firmly at the crossbeam. The left hand will hold the rope tight until the right is placed on the next back strand and so on, advancing from right to left. The entire slack will be taken up at the end by advancing it until the last round is loosened. The end of the rope will thus be free. A final pull with the left hand on the end of the rope while the right holds the last wind firm will complete the operation.

[*64*]

The distance between stick *e* and upper crossbeam *g* must be sufficient to give free play for the hands in tightening. Less than four inches is too short. From twelve to fifteen inches is more usual, but the distance depends somewhat upon the length of the rope. If it is relatively short the sticks will be closer together, if long, they may be

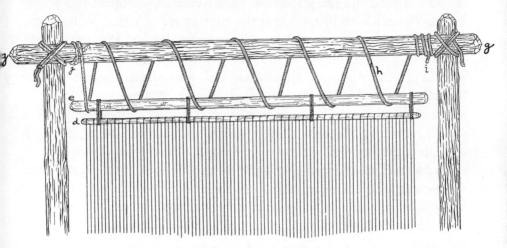

Fig. 3. Variation of rope tieup

far apart. If it is too short, the rope, like many of the other cords, may be pieced.

The tie-up of Fig. 3 is sometimes used. If so, it is more efficient to tighten from left to right or from the back of the loom. The first arrangement is more common. The second does not seem to be closely correlated with left-handedness. For, although left-handed weavers use it, right-handed ones do also. Warp tightening is not a difficult trick to learn, but the Navajo women perform it with such ease and casualness that an outsider merely watching it gets no useful impression of the importance of the whole manoeuver. Only by making and correcting mistakes is the true significance comprehended.

Probably the greatest difficulty in manipulating large rugs occurs at this point. It is met by several devices, two of which may be called mechanical, the other structural. The one chosen will depend upon the time of year, the sort of house a woman lives in, and other considerations. The mechanical adjustments may be used under any circumstances: If the blanket is to be longer than the height of the loom-frame permits, the warp may be rolled carefully around the warp-beam. The stick *e* will be tied at the back of it (Pl. VI,*a*), instead of a few inches above it. As the weaving progresses and the web is laid behind and sewed down to the web-beam, the additional length of warp is unrolled until it is all woven. This arrangement involves careful handling and is at the present day most common.

Rarely used now but common in early days, was the fastening of the warp as in Pl. IV,*d*. This arrangement utilized twice the length of a high loom without the necessary rolling of the extra warp and made warp and web continuous along the front and back of the loom. The warp- and web-beams are close together and the beams at top and bottom, which are our warp- and web-beams, are merely supports to keep the warp stretched, and over which it may move when a change is necessary.

The device I have called structural requires a change in the house or the habitation of the weaver. It means the extension of the loom-frame to such a height as the rug length requires.

This statement means either that the roof must be knocked out of the house or that it must be raised. Actually Navajo houses are not more than ten to twelve feet high, and since many of them are dome-shaped, a maximum of seven or eight feet is all that can be depended on at the side of the house where the loom is placed. Consequently, the weaver who plans to make a large fabric and who wishes to have the entire length of her warp visible will have a loom built in a rectangular shade from which the loom poles may project indefinitely, as did Hastin Gani's Wife (Pl. VI,*b*).

It was necessary to have a ladder outside by means of which the tension-rope could be tightened. A man of the family set up the tall, heavy side posts and laid the bulky crossbeam in place under the direction of Hastin Gani's Wife. After she had woven a portion large enough to take down, it required more than one person to lower the beam. The women can do it if no man happens to be at home, but they look to the men for help if they are available.

It is possible to use the vertically extended loomframe which projects far out of the house or shade only in the summer months when the weather is not too cold. This means at most between May and November first. The period includes the season during which the most rain may be expected. Heavy rains not only interrupt the work but also cause the weaver to see to it that her weaving is protected. The number of those who weave such large blankets as those described is relatively small and they provide the means, casual though they may be, for their own comfort and efficiency and for the protection of their handiwork. It may seem curious to us to rebuild a house or to build a special one for the loom, but the advantages to the designer in judging her space far outweigh the additional labor entailed.

At this point the weaver has all the essential parts of her loom, except one. The warp is strung between the web-beam at the bottom, which furnishes also a simple device for carrying off the finished web, and the warp-beam at the top. The topmost cord or rope furnishes the means of tightening the warp when necessary. The sheds are kept separate by the two reeds which the weaver inserted as soon as they were formed, but as yet there is no means by which they can be thrown or changed. With every part of the loom in place, but with warp not very tight, the worker now proceeds to make a device to regulate the sheds during the weaving process. Where formerly two reeds separated the sheds, she must now supply a harness to make one of the sheds, for if the two stiff elements remained there would be no way for the warps which are pushed back to pass those which have been pulled forward. By dexterously looping the string over the reed the weaver makes the necessary harness (see Lesson 7).

Most hand-woven blankets have no edge binding, but it is a characteristic feature of Navajo rugs. A few only are made without the edge which lends not only finish, but also a decorative value when well done. The edge strands are no real part of the loom. After it is in readiness, the weaver takes the two- or three-ply string which she has ready—it is often the same kind as she used for the edge twining—measures off about six inches more than the length of the blanket, doubles it, and ties one end of the now double cord to the web-beam, twists it by rolling between her palms and ties it firmly to the warp-beam. It is strung from one-half to one inch from the outside warp at each side. All that is necessary now is to tighten the warp with the upper rope and the mechanism is ready for work.

IX *Manipulation*

Although the weaver has arranged the tension rope of the loom (Fig. 2) she has done so only casually, her purpose being merely to attach the moveable part of the loom to the loomframe. Now that she has strung the edge cords and completed the harness, the tension-rope occupies her attention more fully. She makes it tight, watching at the same time the warp-beam to see that it remains parallel to the web-beam at the bottom throughout its length. This may mean that she pulls the rope somewhat tighter at certain points than at others. There is a definite limit to the amount of straightening she can do by this means; that limit is soon reached.

She takes a string and measures the distance between warp- and web-beams at both sides. If there is not more than one-half to one inch difference she will be able to correct it by regulating the rope. It is not likely to be more than half an inch if the weaver is a good one. More than that she detects without measuring. In case the warp is uneven, as it was in my first rug, the worker takes her place before the loom and patiently pulls each warp through its end-twining until no evidence of unevenness in length is visible.

When Marie and her mother strung my first rug, one of the cross-pieces of the warpframe must have moved after the length was measured and before it was fastened. Consequently, it was at least an inch and a half longer at the right than at the left. Marie began a little to the right of the center and pulled each warp carefully until she reached the left edge. After this the measurements at right and left corresponded fairly well. She tightened the rope once more, pulling it somewhat tighter at the left than at the right.

All is now in readiness for the weaving which is accomplished by means of the greatest coördination. Holding her batten as in Pl. V, *a* but nearer the left end, the weaver catches up two warps at a time on it. Before any weft has been laid in, the warps stand in pairs (Fig. 4.) The weaver wants to break up this pairing so she picks up with her batten Nos. 2, 3, drops 4, 5, picks up 6, 7, and so on across. She then turns the batten to horizontal and carries the weft yarn through the shed thus made. With the comb in the position of Pl. V, *b*, she pounds down the weft firmly to the braided edge. She withdraws the batten and takes up on it the warps she previously left behind it, that is, Nos. 1; 4, 5; 8, 9; etc., and repeats the process of laying in weft yarn. Four times across the web, she carries her weft through sheds made

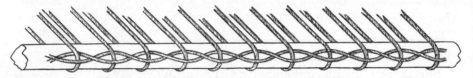

Fig. 4. Warps stand in pairos, edge twining

by alternate pairs of warp. She will not forget to do this also when she puts in the last four rows at the top of her rug. If she does, her rug when finished will show short portions of the warp which will not be noticeable if the weaver breaks up the warp pairing.

From now on the weaving becomes regular. One shed is made by pulling the rod over which the weaver caught the loops, which I shall hereafter call the heald. Pulling this heald Pl. V, *d* causes every other warp to come forward. When this is done, the rod (heald rod) which forms the other shed must be pushed up to a position nine to twelve inches above the heald. The weaver, holding her batten as before, slips it behind the warps thus pulled toward her. At the beginning, before the warp has been stretched much, some of the fibers of those strands which are to move forward will stick to those which ought to remain back. The weaver must always watch that she does not get the wrong strands in front of her batten, but at first it is more difficult to separate the threads than it is later when the fibers have worn off.

PLATE V

[a]
Position of comb and batten for inserting batten

[b]
Position of comb for pounding weft, top view

[c]
Same as b., with hand turned upward

[d]
Pulling heald

[e]
Inserting batten in shed

PLATE VI

[a]
Warp-beam with extra warp rolled under

[b]
16-foot loom

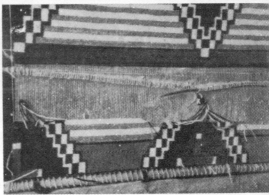

[c]
Blanket turned upside-down so weaver can judge center

[d]
F. Double-faced blanket, different designs

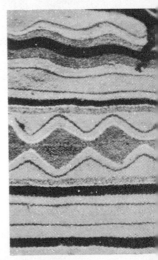

[e]
Design woven in twill ("braided")

The easiest way to do this is to draw the back of the tips of the fingers of the right hand lightly across the warp before pulling the heald forward. Now instead of placing the batten in the shed warp by warp, she slips it easily through the shed. Before bringing it to horizontal she takes up one of the double edge strands on it. If she is weaving from right to left, for example, she takes one of those at the left; if from left to right, one of those at the right. She now moves the batten from vertical to horizontal, thus making a space as wide as the batten through which she may carry her weft yarn. Since she is likely to be making a border, it will be the same color all the way across and she will have it wound on a reed which she will throw from one side to the other.

While she was placing the batten in the shed she held her comb loosely turned down out of her way, as in Pl. V, e. Now that the shed is made, she carries the yarn through it and with a deft turn brings the comb to the position of Pl. V, b, the position necessary for pounding down the weft. She allows the comb to lie freely in position, the motion, like that of hammering, being that of a free wrist. Since the motion is down, the impact comes on the inside of the lower thumb joint. If the comb does not hurt this joint, the weaver is either not holding it correctly or not pounding down the yarn hard enough. So think my teachers at least. But Hastin Gani's Wife takes the impact on the fleshy part of her hand between her thumb and first finger. I have tried this position but have not become accustomed to it. The motion must be free, but firm and strong. At seeing a comb brought down feebly a Navajo remarks "Yego!" which means "Do it hard!" "Don't spare your strength!" She could "show" you but doubtless could not "tell" you that strength can never make up for stiffness.

The weft is pounded down neatly. The weaver removes her batten and pushes the heald rod which forms the second shed close to the loops of the heald. By so doing she forms the second shed and the batten is again inserted. The warps regulating this shed are not so likely to stick to those making the first shed, so that the flick of the fingers is hardly necessary. Weavers, however, often use it so automatically that they do it whether it is needed or not. The first weft was laid from right to left; hence, the edge strand at the left was taken on the batten. The yarn will be carried from left to right this time so that the edge strand at the right is flipped over the wide stick before it is turned to horizontal. Once more the weft is laid in and pounded down, and the rhythmic unit of motion is complete. If the blanket were of self-color for its entire length, these directions would suffice until the weaving comes to within three or four inches on the top.

The weaving done by the expert, our teacher, seems simple and easy, even as do these few instructions. The reason long hours of practise are necessary to achieve her results is that all these motions must be accomplished at nearly the same instant. The comb must be held at rest, as the batten is inserted into the shed with the right hand; at the same time, the left must be making the shed and carefully keeping every warp exactly in place. In the twinkling before the batten is moved to horizontal the edge strand must be slipped onto it, and as soon as it is turned, the comb is shifted from its position of rest to the position for pounding.

During the process of pounding, the left hand is momentarily idle except as it helps in regulating the tension of the weft which is being laid in. In developing any skill, it can hardly be said that any element of the process is more important than any other since the result depends upon a fine adjustment of each of the contributing factors at exactly the moment and in exactly the order needed. So each position and movement, no matter how minor it may seem, must be carefully taken and timed so as to produce the satisfactory web desired. Differences exist, however, in the effects which awkwardness and inexperience will have.

If, for example, I do not hold my comb properly, but lay it down when throwing my sheds and inserting the batten, I shall have to hunt for it, or at least pick it up, when I am ready to pound down the yarn. Nothing in the completed rug will show I did this; it will remain only a matter of inefficiency. If, however, in pulling the heald, I allow two strands to come forward where only one belongs and do not correct it, my rug will always show a mistake where the weft lies over two warps instead of one. From the point of view of the end product, then, it is more important to watch out for certain errors; the others will take care of themselves as time and attention lead to expertness.

The two matters of the greatest importance and most difficult to achieve are securing the proper tension and making straight edges. The two are closely related and, combined, determine the difference between a good and a bad rug. At all times the warp should be tight. At the beginning of the weaving it must be tightened frequently, sometimes after only three or four rows of weft have been laid.

The principle upon which tapestry weaving is based is that none of the warp shows; it is essentially a weft technique. For this reason, weft is usually coarser than warp; in the case of Navajo weaving, it is coarser because much more loosely spun. For the same reason, too, it is of the greatest importance that the weft settle down between the warps loosely enough so as to fill the space nicely, but not so loosely as to make a loop. Thus, in Fig. 5, *a* lies correctly; its thickness is just sufficient to squeeze through the warps and fill the space. The weft *b*, on the other hand is too tight; it allows none of its thickness to remain in the spaces between the warps, and consequently they must show. The tendency of the beginner is to pull the weft too tight, just as the novice does in knitting or crocheting. Call her attention to the fact that she has done so, and she compensates by leaving the yarn too loose, so that there will be more than enough to occupy the warp space and a loop will

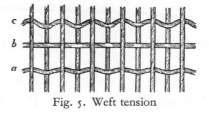

Fig. 5. Weft tension

result as in Fig. 5 c. The loop is not often on the side toward the weaver, for this she will see and correct; it is likely to remain on the opposite side.

The learner will at first be so taken up with the handling of her tools and healds that she will not notice the fact that each row she lays in is becoming imperceptibly tighter. This is something which happens even to excellent weavers and is the reason why few Navajo blankets are exactly the same width throughout the entire length.

Although the weaver-to-be, because of inexperience, cannot notice the narrowing of her web until it has gone on for some time, she will nevertheless have one clue to the tightening. That is, the warp will show in small patches.

One cause for tightness is, strangely enough, loose warp. Perhaps tightening the warp will be sufficient correction. It is more likely that it will not be enough, for the weaver is doubtless not inserting the weft properly. There are two ways of laying it in, one by means of the reed which takes the places of a shuttle, used when wide spaces of self-color are being woven. More commonly, a small quantity of yarn is rolled in a loose ball and simply carried through the sheds as far as that particular color should go. If there is a narrow design, the yarn will be only five to ten inches long and it will hang down at the edge of the pattern for which it has been used. Good weavers never use large quantities of yarn. Beginners often take rather large balls of it or wind a great deal on the reed. The circumstances are the same as those of needlewomen. A beginner always takes a long thread and many of her difficulties come from its knotting or catching into clothing or furniture.

Joining yarn in Navajo weaving offers no problems, or hardly any. It is better to allow the end of the weft to lie at least a few warps in from the edge. If the yarn runs out, the weaver merely pounds it down where it ends—except at the very edge—and lays in a new piece so that it overlaps a little (Fig. 6). If the length should be exhausted

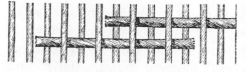

Fig. 6. Piecing weft within blanket

at the edge, she will manipulate it so that a fold-back of yarn comes there instead of the ragged end, as in Fig. 7. With a little judgment and an eye for smoothness joining the yarn will cause no difficulty.

Now that all processes have been described, I shall pause to warn the weaver about the regulation of the weft. It should be laid in the shed diagonally and pounded down from the *bound* end toward the *free* end. The loose end should never be held except to guide it slightly. Another method is to tuck the loose weft down at intervals with the point of the comb, as in Fig. 8, and take up the slack of the big loops evenly between the intervening warp spaces. This is really an interpolation of slackness which gives excellent results. Whichever way is chosen to make the weft sufficiently loose, the action of the comb is of prime importance. An effective weft position may be secured by working the comb with a slight firm twist from the bound end of the yarn toward that which is free. Slow motion: set end of comb at bound end of yarn at about a 45° angle and move it along the arc until its teeth all rest on the finished web and repeat. This motion of the comb should always be used in addition

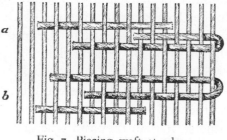

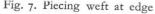

a

b

Fig. 7. Piecing weft at edge

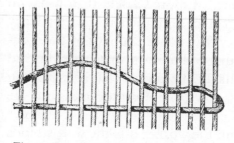

Fig. 8. Inserting weft, yarn tucked down

to the other methods of setting weft. It is best and most efficient, but difficult indeed to describe. I had thumped along awkwardly for days not knowing of its existence. At a particular moment one day. I did not know of it; the next moment I did. Marie could "show" it—the motion is imperceptible to the sight—I doubt if she knows she makes it.

Any or all of the above devices may be used by a given weaver, who, if experienced, sees at once when her web begins to pull in. To guard against tightening she does not carry her yarn through a wide distance before beating it down; perhaps six or eight inches may be the maximum, especially if it is inserted with the fingers. It does not take longer to beat it in instalments than all the way across. Of course, for long spaces the use of the reed makes up in efficiency for the additional caution expended in the pounding.

Suppose that the weaver *thinks* she is laying the weft carefully enough so that it does not pull, but sees nevertheless that some warps, at the end of her rug, let us say, stand much closer together than others, or than they did when she began her work. She knows that her warp is tight and evenly stretched. The close proximity of the warps will tell before her eye detects the deceitful narrowing of the web, that her weaving is too tight. My first blanket required all the possibilities for correction, I am sure.

If the weaving seems to draw in for only a row or two, it may be corrected by setting the weft somewhat more loosely than usual on top of the tight place. This will correct only the slightest tendency toward drawing it in, and its efficacy may be seen at once by the spacing of the warps which will be normal and uniform once more instead of narrow. If, however, as is more likely, the tautness has been gaining imperceptibly for four, five, or six rows, more drastic measures are necessary.

With the pointed end of the comb the worker lifts the weft strands from their places for about five or six rows so that each stands apart along the warp, far above its proper position when finished. The next motion shows how much strain the warp must be able to bear. Grasping the comb by the end having teeth, she runs the point of it firmly along the warp which shows between the rows of the weft which has been lifted up—hard! She presses it as hard as she can as she runs it along several times. Then she turns the comb to its usual position and pounds down the weft once more. If she has not been too gentle in spreading the warp, it no longer shows, and the various strands are more generously spaced than they were before. If she lays her next weft row correctly, the tension may be released and perhaps her troubles are over for the nonce.

There are two other possible corrections for overtight warp. One of the strands at the point of greatest constriction may be simply cut out. If all of these suggestions fail, it is possible to tie a string into the web just below the point of greatest tautness—it is most likely to come at one end or the other—and lasso it to the upright of the loomframe. All of these devices were necessary for my first blanket. I was humiliated at the fact, but had I not made the errors I should never have known how to correct them. With silent satisfaction I noted that an expert weaver at Thoreau had tied her web to the loom upright because it was pulling in.

Up to this time the attention of the learner has been occupied by many things—the holding and managing of the implements and loom, the insertion of the weft, piecing it when its length is exhausted. With all this she may even have had some opportunity to regulate the weft and to correct some tendency toward tautness. By this time another fault will be apparent. The stripe will not be straight; it is lower in the center than elsewhere; indeed there may be several scallops.

A depression extending over a long or short distance may be readily corrected. Instead of carrying the next row of weft all the way across, the worker carries it only as far as the low place in the weave. She changes the sheds and carries it back as far as necessary, perhaps only to the opposite end of the depression. She is then ready to start in where she left off, but there will be an extra row in the portion that was too low (Fig. 9). A thread must always be carried *over* and *back* to complete a row in this kind of weaving. In other words, a row is not complete in design unless all sheds have been used. If this is not done, the weaving becomes confused, for the alternation of the sheds is lost and more than one row of weft will come in a single shed.

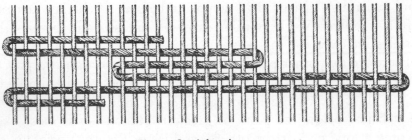

Fig. 9. Straightening a row

If the weaver has caught up the unevenness of the stripe at once, this extra row will straighten it properly. If she has let it become too marked, she will weave a complete row next and lay in an extra weft after that. The Navajo yarn is uneven and it may chance that a thick portion may come at *just* the right spot to fill in properly, in which case nothing more need be done. But the chances are just as good that a thin spot may meet a thin spot for several rows and then it will be necessary to "fill in".

For the method of filling-in here described the batten is used to make the sheds, for the space covered is more than three inches. It differs from regular weaving only in that it does not go entirely across the web.

If, however, the space to be straightened is only a few inches, as wide as the length of the weaver's index finger, let us say, she may leave the batten vertically in the shed she used last. Then, on her left forefinger she takes up the threads forming the shed opposite the one in which the batten lies, and with the right passes the weft through this shed, allowing it to return to its previous position through the shed made by the batten. The dexterity with which the Navajo women make the correction in this way is amazing and unless one is over-attentive it will escape notice or the purpose will be missed entirely. The learner has the idea that only *her* web becomes crooked, that the Navajo woman does not have the same difficulty. The latter sees the unevenness as soon as it appears and therefore corrects it in one deft row. The novice is likely not to sense its presence until it requires two or three rows of filling in.

Aware of all the fine points I have here outlined, and controlling all factors, the Navajo weaver has woven nearly half of the small rug. She has tightened the warp at ever-lengthening intervals, until at this stage she not only finds her warp tight enough but she must even pull hard on her heald to throw the shed. One of the warp strands is holding by only the merest fiber. She inserts her batten, and snap! it has torn. Because this is only a small rug she has used warp which is not up to her usual standard, some of which was given her. Warp would be perfect and manipulation expert, if no strand tore during the weaving of an entire blanket. But even reasonably good warp should not tear so soon, before the rug is half finished. It has not become at all tight compared with the tension it must bear before it is entirely woven. The weaver will be bothered frequently because of this weakness before she is through.

If the tear is not too close to the web, she merely ties in a piece of new warp, making a small tight square knot at each end of the piecing. The knots can later be covered satisfactorily by the heavy weft. If the tear is so close to the web that there is no possibility of tying the lower end, the worker ties a long piece of warp to the torn strand and carries it to the web-beam, where she fastens it firmly by sewing it with a sacking-needle into one of the cords which fastens the warp to the beam. This warp strand now extends from the warp-beam over the finished web and ends at the web-beam. If the strand passed through a heald loop before it tore, it must do so now. If it has escaped the edge braiding at the top, the loose end must be pushed through it with a slender reed or a sacking-needle. One row of weft will bring it into the proper position relative to the other warp strands.

X Continuation of Weaving

When the elements of plain weaving have been mastered (and they must all be put into operation at once), the operation continues with little change at least until half of the blanket or more has been woven. The weaver will be engrossed in perfecting first this part of her task, then that, and bringing them all into coördination. Every effort will reward her, for it will show in her rug which is becoming ever more nearly perfect. If the first blanket is striped, the only difference between it and self-color is in the change of weft color. The weaver should take care that the stripe is straight before introducing a new color, but she should always try to keep her weaving straight.

When a blanket even two and one-half feet long is half finished, it will be difficult for the weaver to reach it easily if she sits on the floor. She may raise her seat by sitting on a blanket or box. Soon, however, it becomes uncomfortable to reach so high. She then loosens the tightening rope and lets down the moveable part of the loom. At this point she can measure the center of her blanket to see if it is exactly the width at the end where she began. More often than not, it is a little narrower.

The worker now uses her sacking-needle again. She lays the finished web in a fold behind the web-beam and sews it to the cords which secure the rug to the stick. She then ties up the loom and works at floor height once more. Most Navajo blankets have a kind of shadow stripe or fold which is always visible no matter how old they become. This is due to the sewing-down at this particular stage of the weaving. All modern looms have some means whereby the web-beam carries off the fabric; the Navajo method is only a makeshift and leaves what might be called a permanent scar on the blanket. The arrangement of the loom such as Adjiba used (Pl. IV, d) prevents this. One wonders why it is not more frequently used. The answer must be that the Navajo do not mind the marks made by sewing.

[81]

Pl. VI, *c* shows a clever manipulation which enabled the weaver to see how her design could be completed. Generally, the weaving is carried to within a few inches of the end and there finished. Alice Curley, however, who made this blanket, when she had finished more than two-thirds of the weaving, simply turned the whole blanket upside-down and finished her design so that she could join the weaving at a stripe. It is much easier to finish the weaving with self-color than with a design.

The position of the rug is now such as entails a change in the loom. It is much lower than before. Fastening it requires either that a much longer rope be used to tighten it, or that the upper beam be lowered. Rope is not usually plentiful, so the second expedient is common since the upper beam of the loomframe can be attached just as easily at a low point as at a high one.

If the rug is a small one (less than two feet), the warp will become uncomfortably tight even before it is half woven. If it is larger, this will occur somewhat later but at least before the weaving has advanced three-quarters of its length. The weaver uses one of her narrower battens when it becomes difficult to pull the heald forward. If she does not do so, the batten will snap from horizontal to vertical, often when her fingers are in the sheds. The stinging rap they receive is by no means pleasant. There are two reasons for this: one, that the warp is tight, a matter that cannot be remedied although the smaller batten will help; the other, that the angles formed by the harness and the batten with the warp do not correspond. Experience shows how the batten may be placed so that it will not snap too often, or at least, not on the fingers.

The weaving becomes still tighter and now a thinner heald rod may supplant the one the weaver has been using. This will make considerable difference in the ease of manipulation, but the relief will not last long for the unwoven space becomes ever tighter. We see the weaver proceel to within four inches of the top of her web. She can no longer insert the reed which serves as a shuttle, but neither can she pass her fingers through the shed with ease. Moistening the end of the yarn slightly, she catches it on the rough end of the reed, gives it a little twist and pushes it through the shed. From now on, she will use the reed more like a beading-needle than like a shuttle.

The weaving advances more and more slowly as the weaver approaches the top. She increases her efficiency by pushing the healds down and weaving from the bottom up. She does not forget that four widths or two rows should be made through sheds made by paired warps, the pairs not corresponding to the way they normally stand. After she has set them by picking the warps carefully with the narrowest of her battens, she again uses her healds. But now, whenever she throws a shed, she inserts a weft at the top of the web already woven and another at the very top of her warp. She is using a small, slim comb and presses, rather than pounds, the first weft down, then firmly pushes the second one up.

When only an inch or even less remains unwoven, she pulls the heald out of its loops and winds up the cord which formed them, leaving only the heald rod to form one shed. For some double rows, that is, one at top and one at bottom, she uses this shed and makes the other with her batten. Finally, she pulls out even this which is no longer thicker than a wire, perhaps *is* a wire, and really darns in the rest of the woof. At this point Maria Antonia used a short umbrella rib, for she could thread the yarn in its eye. Some women use a sacking-needle but the umbrella rib is better because it is thinner and flatter. The yarn must be pressed up with great force. The slim comb sometimes slips, causing the knuckles to rub violently and painfully against the warp-beam. The skilful worker realizes this possibility and avoids it.

Now it is possible to carry the weft through only two or three inches of the width of the rug at a time. Consequently, the worker completes the weaving for this short distance. Many blankets and rugs are loosely woven at this point and their warp shows enough so that an expert can tell this is the end made last. But Maria Antonia and her daughters were most insistent that this final weaving be done closely. When I was sure not another strand of yarn could be forced in, Marie or Atlnaba calmly wove in at least six more!

When she is satisfied she can get no more in, the weaver will have two rows at last in the same shed. Then, with the sacking-needle held concave side down, she catches it into the upper and lower parts of the web with vigorous pressing and pushing so that the join is hidden. If the weaving is close and the gap thoroughly concealed, the effect will be no different from that where two strands of weft are used in evening up a slight concavity. Inch by inch the weaver has made her way across this tedious bit until finally the weft meets from top to bottom and from right to left.

She is ready to take the rug off the loom. She loosens the tension-rope and winds it up. The rug falls down. She pulls out stick *e*, unties the loose strings *f*. She cuts such warps as have been sewed to the web-beam and patiently pulls out the stitches that fasten the surplus web to it. She loosens the balewire which attaches the moveable loom to the frame. The rug is now free from the loom but still attached to the warp- and web-beams. She unwinds the binding cords of these after untying the edge cords.

She unties every knot and winds into neat balls to be set aside for the next rug all cords which do not enter into the weaving. Rarely does she throw string away; never does she cut it. We once used for the heald loops some finely respun Germantown which Maria Antonia had had for at least twenty-five years.

The rug is thrown upon the ground. It is even and regular. At each corner there is a neat loop and a longish piece of double cord. The loop is the end of the braiding, the cord is the end of the side bindings. With a sacking-needle the weaver sews the ends into a thin tassel with loops the size of the original one. She scrutinizes the rug carefully on both sides. With a sharp knife she cuts the warps, which were pieced, close to the fabric so they do not show. It is possible, although not likely, that a few loops exist on the side of the rug which the weaver could not see. These she will shave off also, making the web as smooth as it can be. When her blanket is finished, she ties it up in a floursack to take to the trader at her earliest opportunity, or to lay aside for a time when she will wish to trade it or give it as a gift at a "sing".

If the rug is like my first one was, uneven and warped-appearing, the edge strings may be pulled so as to improve it slightly. If the edge is extra bad, there is one more hope for improvement. The rug may be buried in damp sand for several days when the rainy season comes on. When it is taken out, the edges may be pulled once more and the shape will be somewhat improved. One can never expect a really good rug to come out of one so irregular as to need this treatment; it will merely be "not quite as bad as it was".

XI Pattern

In surveying the vast gamut of Navajo blankets and rugs it is difficult to believe that all but one of the effects of ordinary weaving, even the most elaborate, are based on three quite simple design-elements, which may be varied as to composition, but which remain fixed technically. The learner who knows how to make these three elements—one has two variations—will know all the fundamentals a Navajo woman knows. The genius and taste of the worker will determine how they will be combined for the final effects. There are, of course, other patterns which depend on warp manipulation but this is the weave most commonly found in trade. I shall describe the "fancy" or saddleblanket weaves later.

The general admonition of working in design applies more particularly to a composition of elements, but must be kept in mind in executing even the simplest: *The weaver must keep the composition of the entire rug surface in her mind, but she must see it as a huge succession of stripes only one weft strand wide.* It matters not how ideal her general conception may be, if she cannot see it in terms of the narrowest stripe, meaning a row, of properly placed wefts, it will fail of execution. Because Maria Antonia and Atlnaba have the general and the detailed kinds of vision, they never fail in executing even the most intricate compositions; because Marie lacks complete coördination of these two views of her work, she almost never gets exactly what she has in mind when she starts to weave, as she herself admits. This does not mean that her rugs are not excellent. It means simply that her control of composition is not complete; that, although she may achieve an admirable design, it may not be exactly the one she had in mind.

This, the broadest and must fundamental principle of design weaving, although habitually employed, is almost certainly not realized by the weavers themselves. It is brought under control only after long

[86]

practise. Weavers who are clever at changing their designs after they have been started may be successful without this control; they will never become the adepts who lay out the large sandpaintings, which must be exactly like the copy.

In weaving tapestry patterns it is of prime importance to keep in mind the manipulation of strands in the proper *direction*. If the weaving is from right to left, all threads must hang free at the extreme left of the pattern each is forming when the row is complete; if it is from left to right, they must hang free at the right. All the strands of the row must have the same relative position, there is something wrong if the number is anything less than the whole in either direction. Let us suppose that all the strands are hanging loose at the right of each design-element. On the next row the weaver begins with the loose strand nearest the left, carries it through the left edge, again takes up the one nearest the left which has not been carried through the warp, and so on until the right side of the rug is reached. In weaving the stripe or self-color she was taking a single color from right to left. We may think of this single color as being broken up into many strands with the same manipulation, strand carried from right to left, but the row begun with the one farthest left. In the reverse direction the same principle holds; the thread is moving from left to right, the worker begins with the strand nearest the right. This is important in order to secure the proper Navajo join, which is really only a substitute for a lock. It may be true that a difference in the direction of manipulation would allow for a better lock, but we are learning Navajo weaving, and if the Navajo do not use it, it is not necessarily "better", at least for them.

When I learned to weave, I drew a pretentious design for my second rug (Fig. 10). It was saved from complete disaster by the fact that my teachers wanted the result to be as near perfect as possible. Because my design was faulty, and because Marie made a mistake at the very

Fig. 10. Design proposed for my first rug

beginning, I learned all the design-elements when making the first one. Fig. 11, *a, b,* suggest arrangements in which all the technicalities of design used by the Navajo are present. Furthermore, they appear in the order described below. The amateur in trying out any one of these patterns will start her rug with stripes of self-color, which will continue for a space sufficient for her to understand coördination, tension and straightening. She will then take up successively each design-element, and it will be the only one to occupy her mind for the space in which she uses it. If she follows these suggestions, her first blanket will embody all the necessary requirements of weaving.

The elements, from which all elaborations are made, are the horizontal stripe which the weaver has already mastered, the obtuse-angled triangle, the vertical stripe or line which is achieved in two ways, and the more nearly equiangular triangle. In the total of three I do not count the horizontal stripe, because if one cannot make that, she cannot do this sort of weaving at all. Whether we have a stripe or a background is a quantitative matter only; it depends on where we begin or leave off.

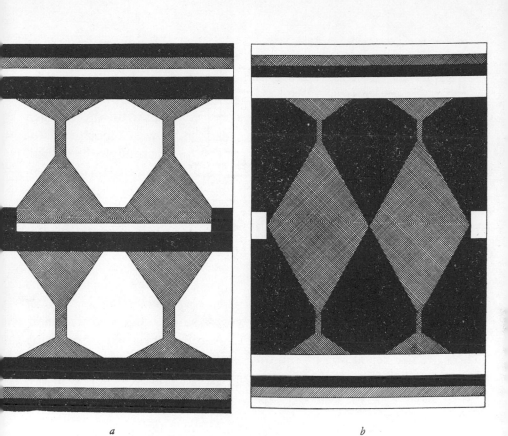

a   b

Fig 11, *a, b*. Designs including all elements

1. Diagonal line of 40⁰ inclination

There are only two types of diagonal lines used by the Navajo in their weaving, the less steep of which makes an angle of approximately 40⁰ with the horizontal. Let us say, for example, that a red line is to lean toward the right, and one to the left, on a black background,

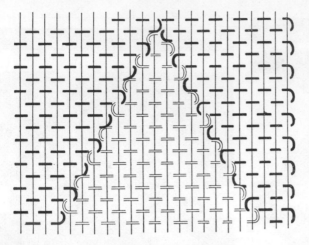

Fig. 12. Line of 40° inclination

forming a triangle as in Fig. 12. At the left the black weft will be carried one warp farther to the right in each row. At both sides of the triangle the red will lose warp on each row, and the black at the right will take up one warp toward the left as it advances row by row.

The effect of this lock, the one most common in tapestry weaving, I believe, is a smooth line sharply differentiated from the contrasting color. Another effect is that of a tiny hole, its size depending on the thickness of the weft yarn. The reason for the hole is the fact that the two opposing loops, one of each color, turn back to their respective fields in the space between the same two warps.

This is the lock which is used when the weaver cannot cover the entire width of her rug in one throw of the shed. If a wide blanket is held up to the light, one can see diagonal lines made of tiny holes which show the way in which the weaver apportioned the space she could reach easily. This shadow line is not a fault. The Norwegians exploit it by using, even exaggerating, it at the line of design and thereby achieve beautiful effects. Strangely, the Navajo have never done so. They always avoid ending a portion of weaving less wide than the whole at a diagonal design line. This is merely habit; it is impossible to tell why they should have developed such a custom rather than one which would allow the artistic use of a technical necessity. If, on such rugs as have designs formed of diagonal lines, they wove only as far as the design, and later filled in the rest of the background, the effects of the mis-matching of self-color which I have previously deplored (p. 32) would not be nearly so marked. The fact remains that they never use the suggested method.

2. *Vertical Stripe*

There are two ways of making the vertical stripe, each depending upon the type of lock one chooses. The width of the stripe must first be determined. It cannot be less than three warps wide.

(a) One way in which the stripe may be made is by interweaving the two contrasting colors on the same warps (Fig. 13). The weft from each side of the stripe will loop about the same warps as those forming the stripe, so that there will be an alternation of colors always over the two binding warp strands. The effect is fringed.

It is more difficult to get a stripe straight this way than by method (b), especially if it is only three warps wide, because the same weft wound about the same warps with no variation exerts an additional pull upon the warps which must constantly be overcome. As a consequence, the few warps involved show a tendency to separate themselves from the others by a wider span than is desirable. A skilful worker has no more trouble in keeping these warps properly spaced than she has with other technical difficulties. There are two advantages which perhaps outweigh the extra care necessary to keep the stripe straight: first,

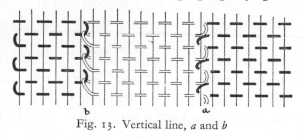

Fig. 13. Vertical line, *a* and *b*

the fringed effect may give a softer, and therefore more artistic effect; second, the weaving feels much smoother where one color joins the other than it does if method (b) is used.

(b) When this method is used, the weft colors are actually interlocked. It involves change of direction in working. Ordinarily the weft colors are all carried in the same direction, that is, toward the side opposite that where the last weft strand placed hangs in the edge twist. That weft color is first carried toward the side in which the weaving is progressing. For example, if the weaving has been carried to the left, the leftmost strand has been carried through the edge twist at the left. After the shed has been thrown the weaving progresses to the right, beginning with the weft color that is nearest the right.

Suppose now that there is to be a border, that is, a vertical stripe at the right made by method (b). Before carrying the first strand to the right (and through the edge twist), bring the second design strand over and let it fall over the loose end of the first as in Fig. 13, *b*. Then take up the first strand to the right and carry it through as usual. The result will be a crossing or interlocking of the weft strands in the space between the warps.

If the whole design consists of vertical lines, or vertical lines made by method (b) combined with horizontal ones, the direction of the weaving will be consistent. In the example just cited, it will be regularly from right to left on one row, beginning with the strand nearest the *left*. For the next row, left to right, the weaver will begin with the strand nearest the *left*, and so alternate the direction of the weaving and the strand which she uses first.

If the design of the blanket involves other methods of interlocking together with this one, which is more than likely, she will have to pay attention so as to carry the weft strands across in such an order as to secure this lock in every other row.

Many women combine methods (a) and (b) in their weaving; the latter is used most often for borders. I have several rugs on which vertical stripes have the (a) lock on one side and the (b) on the other. There is a slight difference in effect, the (b) lock makes a smooth, rather than a distinctly fringed, finish. The difference between the two can be detected quite readily by the way the stripe feels; method (b) causes a pronounced ridge not felt at stripes made by method (a). Some women do not like this ridge. However, the differences are so trifling as to make the choice one of taste or preference, rather than one of wear or artistry except of the most subtle kind.

3. Diagonal line of 52.5⁰ inclination

Whereas the line of 40⁰ inclination is made by advancing the color one warp each row in the direction of inclination, the steeper diagonal line of 52.5⁰ inclination is made by looping the color twice over the same warp each time (Fig. 14). If the method described as No. 1 were used to accomplish this, the hole would always be twice the width of the weft yarn in diameter, a size much too large for Navajo taste. Besides it would constitute a point of weakness in every case, so that the rug would be flimsy and loose instead of strong and compact.

The method is theoretically the same as that used to make the vertical line by method 1 (a), and the fringed effect is the same. The

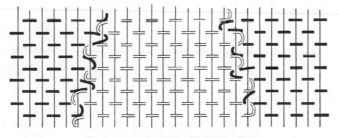

Fig. 14. Line of 52.5⁰ inclination

fact that the work is on a diagonal brings in some complications not noticed in making the straight line. The cue may be taken from the sketch. The weaver may test the accuracy of her work by seeing to it that each color is looped over each warp twice, and only twice, before it advances or recedes. This requires some visual anticipation for she must think of the warp in terms of the one over which the succeeding row is looped. If she is careful about this, the following caution is not for her.

I had more trouble learning to weave this element than with any other. The reason is that I watched the position which the warps at the sides of the triangle assumed. I expected them to be the same every two or at most every four sheds (one or two rows). The exact relationship between warps and weft is not repeated until eight sheds have been thrown, that is, until four rows have been made. The following letters show the position of the end warps no matter how wide the triangle may be. The letter *u* means the warp is *under* the weft, *o* that it is *over*:

warp at left		warp at right
u	... ...	u
o	... ...	o
u	... ...	u
u	... ...	o
o	... ...	o
u	... ...	u
o	... ...	o
o	... ...	u

The Fuzzy Blanket

The "fuzzy" blanket, soft and wooly like an animal's pelt, is one of the simplest to make (Pl. VIII, *a*). Its effect depends more on

PLATE VII

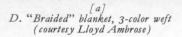

[a]
D. "Braided" blanket, 3-color weft
(courtesy Lloyd Ambrose)

[c]
3-unit diamond, 3-color weft
(courtesy Lloyd Ambrose)

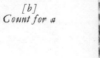

[b]
Count for a

PLATE VIII

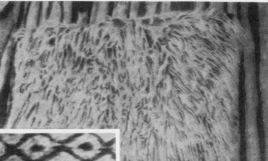

[a]
Fuzzy blanket

[b]
5-unit diamond, 2 sheds light,
one dark

[c]
E. Large diamond,
3-color weft

[d]
7-unit diamond alternating with
braided (b, c, and d courtesy
Lloyd Ambrose)

materials differently prepared than on manipulation of design-elements, for it has no real design. The yarn for this blanket should be coarse and softly spun. Besides the weft yarn there should be at hand a large number of tufts of the long, wavy hair of the Angora goat. These should be carefully selected for softness, color (as white as possible), and regularity.

After the materials are ready, there is little new to learn about the weaving and nothing at all difficult. In the usual way a space about 2-3 inches long is woven of self-color. This will be a little less than the size of the tuft of goat-hair which will hang down over the foundation weaving. In the next row, after sending the weft across, insert one end of a tuft for a few inches and allow the rest of it to hang down just as the weft strands for design usually hang. The difference is that they will remain loose like this; they will not be taken up and interwoven. The insertion of the bunches is repeated at intervals as close as possible. The wooliness and softness of the blanket depend on their number and the evenness with which they are placed. After a row has been laid—along the same shed as the last weft—the shed is thrown and another portion of plain weaving is laid in as before. The tufted rows are repeated at regular intervals for the entire length of the blanket.

The position of the wooly bunches can be seen easily as the blanket grows, and there is no particular difficulty in this weaving. Probably the main reason why it is not very commonly seen in trade is lack of materials. It is not easy to secure as many of the regular-sized bunches of goat-hair as are necessary for even a small-sized rug. I have seen rugs of this sort partly made of yellowish or yellow tufts but they are not nearly as attractive as the white ones. Otherwise, there is little cause for their scarcity. Buyers like them; they are easy to make because the yarn is coarse and therefore quickly spun; the weaving, for the same reason, is quickly done.

Blanket with Scalloped Edge

The blanket with the scalloped edge is not made nowadays, or, if it is, it is extremely rare. There is only one change in the manipulation necessary to secure the unique effect of this blanket. The sheds are formed and alternated in the same way as for the horizontal stripe, but instead of inserting the weft horizontally the weaver lays it diagonally. She begins by making a small triangle at the right, advancing the weft

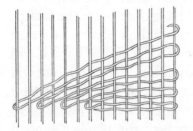

Fig. 15. Detail of manipulation for scalloped edge

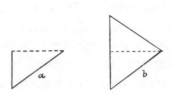

Fig. 16, *a*, *b*. Detail of order of weaving scalloped edge blanket

strands two warps to the left each row (Fig. 15). This is the reverse of the usual triangle which begins with the largest number of warps needed. In this triangle which forms the basis of the diagonal stripe the longest side is made last.

After the first triangle is finished, the weaver continues weaving diagonal stripes all the way across the blanket, advancing them every other warp. As usual, her most important consideration is to get the stripes straight. She may have to do considerable filling-in or evening up in order to make them accurate. But if the initial triangle is straight, there will be little trouble with the other stripes. When the weaving has crossed the blanket once, there will be a band of diagonal stripes of such colors as the weaver selects and of the width she chooses. They need not all be the same. At this stage she has finished half the design unit, for it is really a chevron pattern made in two bands, each composed of diagonal stripes.

The last "stripe" of the first half of the design has really the triangular shape, Fig. 16, *a*. The weaver next makes a triangle at the left by carrying the weft diagonally until she has doubled this triangle so that it appears Fig. 16, *b*. The line in the drawing through the center is merely a shadow line formed by the weft strands of one row meeting those of the other. After this triangle has been woven, the second half of the design will be at exactly the same stage at the left as the first half was at the right when the first triangle was made. The worker now weaves a broad band consisting of diagonal stripes from left to right. Each stripe should be the width of the same color in the first row and should meet it exactly, thus completing the chevron of that color.

The fact that much weft is packed into the end triangles, more than the warp can comfortably hold, is what causes the edge to appear scalloped when the rug is taken down. This kind of edge is not objectionable—it may even be decorative—if the various elements of the design are accurately spaced, and if the "overstuffing" may bulge at the edge. There are, perhaps, more of these blankets which are badly made, than there are of good ones.

The opinion my teachers had of my sample of this kind of blanket was one of scorn. "Somebody did it who didn't know what she was doing," remarked Marie. It happens that this piece which is old and much the worse for wear is not good by any standards except those which make age a fetish. The design is bad, there being practically no matching of the many colors employed, and no balance. When the women made fun of it, considering it as "one huge mistake", I insisted that if the whole thing were a mistake, the scallops would not be as uniform in size as they are along the sides, and what is more, the scallops of one side would not alternate regularly with those of the other. After considerable discussion and thought Maria Antonia said she knew how to do it and would start to make a blanket of the sort. I also thought I knew how to do it.

As is customary with us we started "tomorrow"(the Navajo "tomorrow" does sometimes come). Maria Antonia started to weave. But, to my disappointment, she merely imitated the pattern of the borrowed blanket in the usual technique, making the zigzags accurately enough by setting in a color and at the next row moving it one thread to the left. By this means diagonal stripes were achieved, but they were made up of weft laid horizontally and there were no scallops at the edge.

I protested that the appearance was all right, but not at all like what I was trying to work out. I had decided that the weft was woven in diagonally, so that by the time a row was finished there was too much weft for the warp to accommodate, making a "stuffed" effect. I asked Maria Antonia for the comb. Of course all the women were in curiosity assembled. I wove the way I thought it was, but my diagonal stripe became rounded at the middle. The loom had been strung up temporarily for this try-out in Atlnaba's house and the upper rope was too close to the upper beam to allow for proper tightening. My error was the result of loose warp. However, the idea seemed to be all right.

Ninaba had been weaving a small rug on a loom which was fastened to the same large loomframe we were using. Atlnaba caught my idea at once and started to carry it out on Ninaba's loom, setting it in on top of what the little girl had already done. During the entire procedure she protested quietly but doggedly, and was as persistently ignored by her mother. I was sorry for her, but we were in a hurry and Atlnaba about half acceded to Ninaba's demand, "You have to take it out again."

In order to see if our diagnosis were correct it was necessary to weave a row across in the diagonal fashion we were affecting, and then at least one back with the diagonal in the opposite direction. This Atlnaba did quickly, as is her wont, and when it was finished, although it looked "overstuffed" we took it down to be sure it bulged at the ends. It did.

XII Saddleblanket Patterns

Although designs made by variation of the weft are the most numerous among trade pieces and even in carefully selected collections, they are not, in my opinion, the most interesting of the Navajo weaves. The difficulties involved in making some of the more unusual ones are due to the necessity of concentration rather than to any inherent complexity. Until recently the Navajo have not exploited the so-called saddleblanket weaves, and even now I know of only one region where they do. The Navajo make them primarily for their own use, usually as saddleblankets. Some, though effective, are simple indeed, others are more complicated.

The difference in pattern between these rugs and the others I have described is a difference in the setup of the warp. For some of them only two healds (a looped one and a heald rod) are used, for only two sheds are needed even as in weft weaving. In others four are necessary (three looped, and one rod). I will describe the varieties under letters and names in such cases for which the Navajo have names.

A. "*It is woven*"

The blanket called "it is woven" is as simple to make, and as simple in effect, as its name (Fig. 17).[1] With warp strung in the fashion usual for weft weave, the difference is that two colors alternate in the rows making a simple design of vertical stripes. If, for example, one uses black and red as the

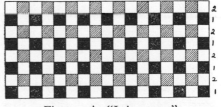

Fig. 17. A. "It is woven"

[1] In the figures which show the counts the white blocks indicate that the weft is under and, therefore, does not show. They do not represent a color.

[99]

weft strands, black is carried across when the heald rod throws the shed, red when the loop heald makes it. This is often referred to as a "beaded" pattern by Whites. The Navajo use it extensively for parts of design in many rugs.

A combination of vertical and horizontal stripes, that is, a simple plaid, may be formed by alternating two colors for a given space and then using some other color. A number of variations may be made upon the theme, but if the vertical stripes are to be unbroken only two weft colors are used.

B. *"Speckled"*

The only difference between the "speckled" blanket, B (Fig. 18), and "it is woven", A, is that two warps are strung on each heald. That

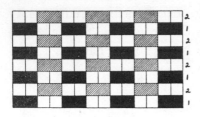

Fig. 18. B. "Speckled"

is, the heald rod holds in place two alternate warps instead of one. The other heald has two warps caught into each of its loops, those two which are not held forward by the other rod. The weaving is an alternation of two weft colors, each thrown, as before, all the way across.

The effect secured by this type of weaving is coarser than that of A. It is really no more "speckled", the "speckles" are merely larger.

C. *Weave with no Name*

The blanket I have lettered C has no Navajo name (Fig. 19). It is somewhat like A and B but three healds are used instead of two and the weaving is done with two colors alternating. This is really a combination of "it is woven" (A) and "speckled" (B).

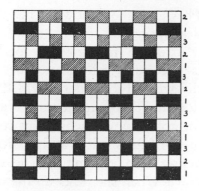

Fig. 19. C

From now on, the number of warps strung on the healds and the number of weft colors will not necessarily correspond so I shall write at the right of the diagrams the number of healds, beginning always from the bottom for my count. For this pattern heald 1 has alternate pairs of warp strands in each loop. Heald 2 has the pair in each loop not taken up by heald 1. Heald rod 3 is laid in with alternate warps over it exactly as it would be for ordinary weft weaving.

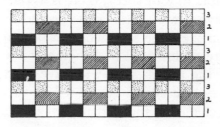

Fig. 20. C

With two weft colors this style appears as Fig. 19. If three weft colors are used it appears as in Fig. 20.

All of the saddleblanket weaves depend for their effect upon the relation between the number of sheds and the number of weft colors used. More often than not, the number of weft colors is smaller than the number of healds.

D. "Braided" (Twilled)

The weave called "braided" is the first of the diagonal patterns I shall describe. Four healds are needed for this weave. The diagram,

[101]

Pl. VII, *b*, shows how the healds are to be strung better than a verbal description.

After the stringing is properly done and the sheds are made, there is a necessary coördination between the order in which the sheds are thrown and the order in which the weft colors are laid. The perfection, and therefore the success and beauty of the blanket, depend upon the accuracy with which this correlation is made and sustained. The order of the sheds is at first: heald 1, heald 2, heald 3, heald 4 (numbering from bottom up). The order of colors is, let us say, black, red, gray. When she picks up the color required to throw it, the worker makes sure the strand is inside any others that may be at the same end. This is done to keep the edge as smooth as possible. It makes no difference which shed is made first or which color of weft she begins with, but after she decides, the sequence of both sheds and weft colors must be kept up.

Since there are only three weft colors to four sheds, there is a complete round of both only every twelve rows. That is, at the end of twelve rows the same color occurs in the same shed where it began, but not before. At this point all three colors will be hanging at the side where the weaving began and the fourth shed will have been used, so that the rhythmic unit is twelve and is composed of two smaller units, the shed unit of four elements, the weft unit of three.

1	2	3	4	1	2	3	4	1	2	3	4
b	r	g	b	r	g	b	r	g	b	r	g

Usually "braided" blankets are made with stripes consisting of diagonals running first in one direction then in the opposite direction (Pl. VII, *a*). The change in direction may be made whenever desired by reversing the order of the sheds and of the weft colors. Whereas, for the first band consisting of diagonal stripes one weft wide, the weaver used the sheds in the order 1, 2, 3, 4, she now has 4, 3, 2, 1. The order of weft colors was previously black, red, gray; it is now red, black, gray. The largest unit is the same in size as before; there is a difference in order of both small units which compose it.

heald   4 3 2 1   4 3 2 1   4 3 2 1
weft color   g r b g   r b g r   b g r b

This is the form of the unit after it is started. The following shows its form at the point where the change of direction is made:

1   2   3   4   3   2   1   4   3   2   1   4
g   b   r   g   r   b   g   r   b   g   r   b

The diagram shows, even as does the sketch of the stitches, that the manipulation is symmetrical above and below the line formed by weft run in shed four at the point where the diagonals are made to reverse their direction.

E. "Large" and "small" diamond

The directions for making the "braided" blanket give the fundamental principles of all the diagonal weaves. The "large" as well as the "small" diamond, are made by regulating the order of four healds, or sheds, and three weft colors. The Navajo distinguish two diamonds, as the title of this section suggests, but they are made the same way. The difference between them and "braided" is in the way the warps are strung. The diagram (Fig. 21) shows the count for "large" diamond; "small" diamond of any size is made simply by taking smaller units.

If the order of the healds is reversed after one entire unit is complete, the effect is as in Fig. 21. If the order of healds is retained, it

Fig. 21. E. Large diamond

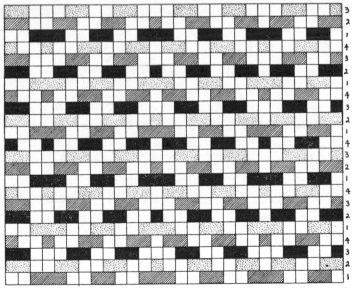

Fig. 22. Horizontal zigzags. Warp for diamond, healds not reversed

is as in Fig. 22. The first is a diamond pattern, as the name of the blanket suggests; the second is an allover succession of zigzags with diamond never completed. It differs from "braided" (Pl. VII, *a*) in that the zigzags run horizontally instead of vertically.

There seems to be no exact point at which a diamond becomes large, but one with eleven units would doubtless come in that category; the units must have an odd number of warps, three is the least which can be used.

When I was teaching my sisters how to string the warp for the diamond weaves, I discovered a simple way to do this without the need of "having my paper tell me". It is possible, too, by this method to place the point of a diamond at the exact center of the blanket. I do not believe, however, that many Navajo women, if any, make their sheds from this point of view. I make the warp at the center of the blanket the center of the diamond. If the diamonds are to be small, I should allow 3, 5, 7, or 9 warps for their width, if large, 13 or more. Since the same principle holds for all I will choose 9 as a unit.

After finding the center warp of the center diamond I take it up on my batten in regulating the warps for heald rod 4. I then take up every other pair of warps on each side of it until I come to a multiple of 9. This time the odd strand will be under and I proceed with two over and two under until the next multiple of 9 is over the batten. When the warps are in this orderly fashion over and under the batten for the whole width of the blanket, I press the batten down to the bottom of the warp as do the Navajo. I can then readily detect any mistake I may have made. If I have made none, or when I have corrected all, I turn the batten horizontally and insert a reed, push it up, withdraw the batten. Since shed 4 is made by the heald rod, which has no loops, it must always be at the top. Otherwise it will bind the warps so that those in the heald loops cannot move forward.

In counting off the warps for shed 3 I find the odd warps of shed 4.

Each will be the center one of three warps which will always be under in this shed. On each side of this center of three warps left under, I again alternate pairs of two until I reach the next multiple of 9. This odd strand will be under on heald rod 4 if the first one was over, or vice versa, but on heald 3 all three strands are under. I repeat the test for accuracy by running the batten to the bottom of the warp. When the count is correct I substitute a reed for the batten and make ready to count off the warps for heald 2.

I do not loop the healds until the counts are ready for all. After the learner has tried this, she will readily understand that waiting to make all the loops for the harness at once may save much labor for, if I have inadvertently overlooked an error, I shall have to repeat only the count on the batten instead of that plus the heald looping.

The healds (or sheds) are paired so that heald 2 is the opposite of 4. That is, if warp 9 is up on 4, it is down on 2. Healds 3 and 1 likewise form a pair which regulate three warps at the center. If heald 3 has three over, heald 1 will have the same three under. Since this is true, all I need do in making shed 2 is to see that such warps as were over on heald 4 are under on this, and that those which were under are over.

I follow the same procedure for heald 1, making the shed it controls the opposite of shed 3.

I will now have four rods or reeds each with the proper strands over and under according to count. I leave the top one, heald rod 4, as it is. I insert the batten in the shed made by rod 3, withdraw the rod and hold it along the outside of the warp and loop as for the simplest weaving but catch 1, 2 or 3 warps into each loop according as they stand forward alone or in groups on the horizontal batten. I repeat this operation for all three sheds and the result is a four-harness loom, ready after tightening for the weaving.

F. *"Woven opposite"* *(Double-faced Cloth)*

It is surprising to hear how frequently laymen and even traders who handle large quantities of blankets, refer to the "braided" and "diamond" weaves as "double-faced" blankets. They do so because the order of the colors is reversed on the two sides. The blankets are, however, no more double-faced than our ordinary carpets or other woven fabrics. If weft of two or more colors is carried all the way through the sheds, even though there be only two sheds and two colors of weft the colors must take up alternate positions on the two sides. Consequently what is red on the face must be black on the reverse.

A truly two-faced or double-faced cloth has entirely different patterns on the two sides, like a steamer rug or like certain double-faced coat cloths. The Navajo can make a fabric corresponding to these although they do not often do so. The few double-faced rugs in existence are generally considered somewhat remarkable, and they vary from simple designs on the face with a plain different-colored reverse to combinations of the ordinary weave with one of the more elaborately strung saddleblanket weaves.

I shall describe one of intermediate complexity, one with ordinary weaving on the side toward the weaver, and a speckled pattern at the back.

For these effects a four-harness arrangement is necessary. It is set up exactly as for "diamond" but naturally with different counts for each heald. Just as the sheds (healds) are paired for the "diamond", so they are for the "double-faced". They may be paired either as 1 with 2, 3 with 4, or as 1 with 3, 2 with 4. I prefer the first type just because it seems to me a little easier to remember a common order than an alternating one in throwing the healds. In this case there are two pairs, each standing for something different. There is a pairing of sheds 1 and 3, one of which is the reverse of the other, that is, those warps which are over on heald 1 are under on heald 3. The same holds for healds 2 and 4. But one pair not the same as that just described regulates the face design, the other the reverse. So that in the example I am giving healds 1 and 2 will, if used with the proper weft manipulation, form the design on the face of the cloth. When alternating colors are run through the entire width of the sheds made by healds 3 and 4, the "speckled" pattern results at the back. The sheds are of course thrown in the order 1, 2, 3, 4, so that two face rows and two reverse rows alternate.

Most weavers say they do not know how to make the "double-faced" blanket, but if you show a woman one with heald 1 paired with 2, and 3 with 4 she will say, "I always use pairs 1 and 3, and 2 and 4." If, on the other hand, you show a weaver (perhaps not the same one) the second arrangement she will be sure to tell you that *she* uses the one I describe here. What they really mean, I suppose, is that either may be used, and that there is little difference if any between the two, and they really do know all about it!

What is important for the weaver to know is that if healds 1 with 2, and 3 with 4, regulate the design, heald 1 will alternate with 3, and 2 with 4 in the stringing. By the same token, if healds 1 with 3 and 2 with 4 form the designs at front and back respectively, heald 1 will pair with 2, and 3 with 4 in the stringing.

Fig. 23 shows how the harness is arranged for the combination of ordinary weaving and speckled. The healds are thrown in the order 1, 2, 3, 4 continually until the blanket is finished. When healds 1 and 2 are forward the design is woven in, when heald 3 is forward the reed shuttle is thrown all the way across with one color, and when 4 is forward, the shuttle with the second color.

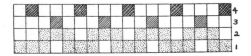

Fig. 23. F. Double-faced: ordinary weave on face, "speckled" on reverse

Usually double-faced rugs are made with ordinary weave on one side and a simple stripe of some sort, ordinary weave or weaves A, B, or C at the back. I have seen several, however, which have ordinary weaving of different patterns, other than stripes, on both sides. This sort of blanket is more difficult to weave than the one involving merely stripes at the back. The reason is that one design must be woven blindly, so to speak; it cannot be seen by the weaver although she has a guide.

I have worked out a count for "braided" on the face and "ordinary" weave at the back. It involves six healds. Theoretically eight might be used in a combination of "diamond" and "braided" or large diamond and small. Practically I have not found it working well because so many crude harnesses are awkward and hard to throw.

[The "doublecloth" to which Amsden refers (p. 62) is a variant of this technique which I shall discuss in Chapter XIV. It is Navajo and is called by the name "it-is-woven-opposite".]

The manipulation for the saddleblanket patterns is not difficult. It is, however, trying as compared with the regulation of the loom and implements for ordinary weaving. Making the harness may be a tedious task, for the warps must be counted off carefully. Mrs. Kinni's-Son showed me how to count them off and string the heald loops. She strung the warp in the usual way over the warpframe but did not separate the sheds with the two rods as we always do for ordinary weaving. After she had attached the moveable loom to the loomframe, she put the rod through the warp with alternating warps upon it, then pushed it to the top. She did this to avoid the confusion caused by the paired loops of the warp at the end.

When I set up one of the "diamond" counts from my notes, I did not do this for I counted my strands at the center where they stand apart in order, but Mrs. Kinni's-Son was sure it was going to be wrong. I do not think she even knew why it was not.

The first blanket she strung for me was "braided". She had no trouble with the first two rods she put in (heald rod 4 and heald 3), but for the third (heald 2) she became confused. She seemed to be proceeding by a method of trial and error. She caught up the strands, then pulled out her batten and tried again. After repeated unsuccessful trials she pulled out the top rods and started all over again. Finally she gave up altogether and had her daughter at it. It had taken her one and one-half hours. Her daughter had the counts ready and the loops made in twenty minutes. It took me the same length of time to make the harness for "small diamond", working, of course, from my sketch.

Later Mrs. Kinni's-Son strung up a large diamond for me. I had supposed her difficulties with "braided" were fortuitous or temperamental, but the same thing happened again. I suppose if her daughter had not been present, she would have persevered until she succeeded. She had set up dozens of these blankets, but she had never generalized the setups so that she could proceed unerringly.

A long time after, I was showing Marie how to make these weaves. We had our loom outside and I tried and tried to make the counts for "braided". I knew how to do it without notes but I constantly made mistakes. I could do no better than give up for the time. Before I attacked the task again, I hung a plain-colored dark blanket behind the loom. After that I had no difficulty. Mrs. Kinni's-Son had her loom against a dark background. I think her repeated failures at different times show that she sensed the counts but had not actually reduced them to rule in her mind. Her daughter had done so.

Mrs. Nanaba Bryan who taught weaving at Fort Wingate said to me when we were discussing the "double-faced", "You better write it down or you'll forget it. This is the way I remember the different kinds." So saying, she unrolled a long narrow moveable loom on which were neat samples with complete harness of all the exceptional warp combinations.

We made a modification of this for Marie. Every time we finished a few inches of one pattern we carried in a string before pulling out the healds. We pushed these to the top of the loom and started in with another style. When Marie's "weaving notebook" was finished, she had a short space of weaving at one end of the loom and at the opposite end the strings which regulate the counts; those for each type were in reverse order to the weaving. This was Atlnaba's idea.

Although Marie never, in the whole time I worked with her, made a generalization herself, she understood and was grateful for all that I made in showing her.

XIII Designing Ordinary Weaves

If we knew the exact process whereby a Navajo weaver comes by her designs, we should have the definition of inspiration. Almost any drawing has the potentiality of stimulating her with the idea for a rug, but the details of the suggestive material will rarely, except in certain tragi-comic cases, appear exactly as they occur in the original. They will be revamped and reassembled so that, unless the weaver tells us, we should seldom anticipate the origin of her composition. Nor does she always need an external stimulus. While she was working on her last rug, suggested perhaps by the wrapper of a "crackerjack" box, another pattern, perhaps with no discernible relationship, may have come to her.

Until quite recently the Navajo women wove all compositions "out of their heads". Most of them still do so. That is, they visualize a design and carry it out. Some like Atlnaba, sure of plan and confident of skill, execute the initial conception unfalteringly. More, perhaps, like Marie, modify the intention as the actuality of weaving shows it to be faulty, out of proportion, or in some other way unsatisfactory.

The most such a weaver allows herself are guides for symmetry and straightness. She ties a short piece of yarn to the central warp. When the rug is only started, with a piece of cord she measures off the center of the length and marks it clearly with a pencil. After she has counted off the number of warps to be used for a diamond, a rectangle, or a triangle and inserted her weft at the bottom, she may count off the corresponding warps at the top and tie a piece of yarn around them loosely enough to allow them to cross when the heald is pulled forward. The initial design will pass out of sight when she sews the rug down at one-quarter or one-half its length. She can look at it as it lies folded behind the web-beam but it will always be out of perspective, and even if she does not sew it down, the key to the exact strands held by the tie of yarn is convenient and makes for exactness.

Nowadays even some middle-aged women are "schoolgirls", that is, they have been to school. They may sketch the general outlines of their compositions on paper but they do not include all details. Those weavers who achieve the good sandpainting tapestries copy faithfully a drawing made by one of their menfolk. Men know the paintings, only a few women do and they are not likely to weave them.

When I was learning to weave designs it was necessary to make a drawing, for I wanted to weave my own design and my teachers wanted me to. The only way whereby they could know what I wanted was by a drawing. My first attempt (Fig. 10), made before I had analyzed the elements of design used by the Navajo, was artistically and technically a failure.

The proportions were bad because a blanket as small as I wanted to make could not accommodate all the detail I tried to get into it. At that I thought the pattern very simple. There were two faults of detail which made it impossible to carry out the design for technical reasons. The sides of the small innermost triangles have an inclination of 40^0, the outer ones have 52.5^0. If the rug were large, there might perhaps be space enough to carry them out but they would not look well. In this one whose width was less than five hands wide it would have been impossible to do so. Furthermore, I should never have designed an incomplete triangle, at least not a hollow one. The result of this whim is evident in Pl.IX, *a* which shows the best result Marie could achieve. I liked the effect of black, white and green stripes on a sandpainting tapestry that Atlnaba finished and decided to use these colors.

The hollow green triangle nearest the center, the white one succeeding it, the black and the next white each have "crowns" or crosspieces. Marie, for some reason, almost certainly because of miscalculation and doubt, stopped off the largest green hollow triangle without this sort of extension. The effect is incongruous. Even if she had made it like the others, all would have been, as they are now, unsuitable and un-Navajo.

Marie did not have enough warp of the kind she started with for this blanket, and had to finish with some that was finer. Instead of allowing for this difference she counted the warps as if they were all of one size, therefore, the design is not centered.

I know of no reason, lest it be my mistake in drawing the concentric triangles of different sorts, why she started the triangle at an inclination of 40°. Even I, who knew naught of laying out a pattern, could see that this would come to its apex long before it reached the center of the rug. The weaving had not progressed far, when Red Point called her attention to the fact. That gave us no pause, we continued as we had begun.

The result was thoroughly unsatisfactory. The weaving was nowhere nearly like the intention, and because the triangle was completed too soon we had too large a space of white at the center. Devoid of inspiration we kept on weaving. I felt that the white space was unbalanced and monotonous, but continued to weave it for some distance, meanwhile considering the possibility of inserting the triangles. Marie agreed with me and we finally put them in, but they have no function in the design.

Our errors taught me two unexpected lessons. My drawing had not provided at any point for a vertical stripe and if we had chosen to be consistent and succeeded, we should have had only one kind of triangle, the one whose base angles are 52.5°. As it turned out, this blanket, though far from satisfactory, involves all the elements used in Navajo weaving.

After considering all phases of the matter, I decided to change my design so that it would be more suitable. When I set up the first blanket of my second summer, the drawing was that of Fig. 24, all to be done in white, black and red. As Marie was away that summer Atlnaba showed me how to proceed. She quite wisely strung the rug a little longer than the former one had been so that the hourglass design could be better accommodated. I had no difficulty with this one.

As I progressed rapidly with this, it seemed to me that the combination of white, black, and red, was too clear, too hard. I resolved, therefore, to soften it with a few gray stripes at the sides. This afterthought was not so long delayed or of such a kind as to be ineffective. Atlnaba was much pleased with it. I had learned many things from the green blanket. One of them was that the pattern would have greater dignity if the stripes at the sides were wider, especially at the middle. The changes were all put into effect; the rug turned out as we planned it.

Fig. 24. Blanket with first design modified

As I wove, Atlnaba made two suggestions, not by way of criticism, but merely saying, "It would be nice this way, too." One was that there be a center triangle of solid gray as in Fig. 26, the other, which greatly appeals to me, that the inner red triangle should have a gray terraced lining inside it as in Fig. 25.

My family had many visitors; all of them were brought to my hogan to see me at work. Maria Antonia's "younger sister" suggested it would be nice to outline all the triangles with a contrasting color just one warp wide. This would mean, perhaps, that the outer red triangle

25. Atlnaba's suggested modification of Fig. 24   Fig. 26. Another suggestion of Atlnaba

would have a gray outline on one side, black on the other, the black might have red and gray, the inner red, black or gray, or both. In making this recommendation she was expressing Navajo favoritism. Many details are outlined, although outlining requires much extra labor; some have as many as three narrow contrasting lines. This phase of style lends an air of great finish.

Outlining is not confined to the woman's art. It is the outstanding feature of the sandpaintings, although at first sight it would seem unnecessary and difficult to achieve. The sandpaintings are in no case easy to make, but no detail, no matter how small, is left out for the sake of expediency. One of the most common designs used in sand-paintings is the rainbow or sunray. It consists of a stripe of red and one of blue, each delicately outlined in white. Pl. IX, *b* shows the succession of lines around the central design called the Sun's-House. Within the lower stripe which is yellow are four Snake "houses", each outlined with a rainbow garland. Each of the four cloud figures at the sides of the Sun's-House has four sun rafts on its surface, they are made in the same way, and each cloud has the same finish. Not only is it necessary to make feathers, in themselves small, with accurate barbs, but each one has a contrasting tip and at its very end, a mere dot of the second color, really a "contrast to the contrast". We cannot be sure that the weaving style grew out of that of the sandpainting because we do not know the age of either, but it seems likely. It is possible, of course, that both grew up together; the style is more pronounced in the religious mosaics.

So common is the use of outlining in weaving that a type of blanket on which it is prevalent is called the "outline" blanket. It is made at the present time east of the Chuskai-Lukachukai mountains, but is by no means confined to that region, nor is this means of finishing a design restricted to a single category of rugs.

Although I myself started making a blanket entirely of stripes, I do not think it necessary to make a whole rug of this motive since the weaver will always have practise on self-color (or stripes). I have, therefore, designed Fig. 11 *a* and *b*, which embody all the elements a weaver has to learn in such a way that she need think of only one at a time. The stripes furnish the initial lesson. After she has made them she will take up the line of 40° inclination, in this case one leaning to right and left on each side of the rug so that triangles result. Before pointing off the triangles she starts a vertical stripe using method (a) (p. 91). The few inches up which it is carried will suffice to show her the problems and she will begin on lines of 52.5° inclination which will form triangles placed in the opposite direction. At the center the pattern is broken by several horizontal stripes (number and color to suit taste of weaver) but I have allowed for a short vertical stripe on each edge to be executed by method (b) (p. 91) more commonly used for borders.

Modifications of various kinds are possible and will suggest themselves to any craftsman. The arrangements here submitted are simple and complete. They allow the learner to concentrate on a single phase of her work. Ultimately, she will have a blanket whose design is not bad, while it is at the same time strictly Navajo.

Infinite variety is secured by the Navajo by weaving representative or realistic designs (see Chap. XVII). A bird, animal, or man is formed by the worker by the use of the joins I have described under line of 40° inclination, vertical stripe (a), or line of 52.5° inclination. In laying in a bird, for example, the difference lies only in the number of rows for which each technical motive is used. In forming a rounded head, let us say, the rows will be made by the same means as vertical stripe (a), but the weft will be arranged so as to advance or recede one or more warps at each row. No matter how detailed or how elaborate a pattern may *look*, the method of manufacture is the same.

I suggest that the weaver master the few technical devices here described. I have tried to save her time by combining them all in one rug; I hope the effect of this blanket will be an encouragement to her. After she knows them her compositions will depend entirely on her own taste, subordinated of course to the technical limitations of her craft.

The Scalloped Blanket

I have shown how the blanket with scalloped edges is made (p. 96). Many of the Navajo women hold the edge for a fault, since they are

PLATE IX

[a]
Blanket resulting
from my first design

[b]
Tapestry of Sun's House sandpainting

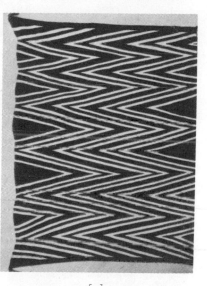

[c]
Blanket with scalloped edges (courtesy
Metropolitan Museum)

[d]
Beginnings of scalloped blanket (courtesy
Metropolitan Museum)

PLATE X

[b]
*5-unit diamond, 2-color weft,
4th heald*

[c]
*"Braided" in 2 colors alternating with
narrow stripes of twilled diagonal*

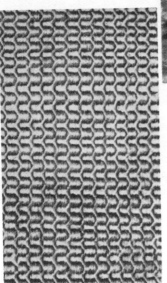

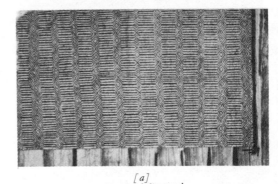

[d]
*5-unit design, 3 colors, 4th heald delayed
(b, c, and d courtesy Lloyd Ambrose)*

[a]
*Bands of diamond
alternating with
bands made
by delaying 4th heald*

not now accustomed to uneven edges. Their ideal is a straight edge, but it is merely a matter of taste and tradition.

Blankets of this type have, however, a major technical weakness at the straight line where the lines composing the chevron meet. Because of the way the join is made — it may be more correct to say, "because of the place where the join is made" — a straight horizontal line has many holes. The join at each warp is really the same as that described for the diagonal line of 40° inclination, but in that case the holes made by the weft loops opposing each other occur along a diagonal. In this, the holes occur along a straight line, since the line woven is diagonal. All of the blankets of this sort that I have seen are old. All which have been exposed to use have torn along these lines of weakness. This cause alone, I believe, is sufficient to account for the lack of popularity of this kind of blanket among Navajo women.

Another reason why it is no longer made may be the effect of the design. If it is carried out out by regular repetition of the initial band unit composed of diagonals, it may be disturbing to the eye (Pl. IX, c). James[1] cites an example of a Navajo man who had woven a blanket with this pattern in a twilled web. Before he had taken it from the loom, a storm with lightning came up. When suddenly the sun broke through a cloud, according to the weaver, it brought the pattern to life. It was as if the lightning played over his loom and he could not be rid of the blanket too soon, so he took it to a trader with the request that he do away with it. It is not difficult to understand how the design may be felt to move; it belongs in the class of designs, such as spirals and triskeles, which take on motion as one views them.

The scalloped blanket may be decoratively effective if the double bands of diagonals which form the chevrons are separated by straight lines. This treatment strengthens it and keeps the zigzags in their place, thus avoiding the disagreeable effect of their motion.

[1] Indian Blankets and their Makers, p. 122.

I have said that my teachers regard this type of blanket as a mistake. I think they are right in one respect, for it may well have originated in an error made by an unskilled weaver. Pl. IX, *d* and *c* illustrate the possible development although I am not sure *d* was made before *c*.

Pl. IX, *d* consists primarily of the ordinary weft weave, but at the centers of the large diamonds of the central part of the blanket the "over-stuffing" is used and at this part of the design there is a large scallop on each side of the blanket. At each end where the diamonds are filled in with stripes the edges are constricted. From this example it may easily be seen how the diagonal weaving which leads to stuffing may be further carried out consistently so as to make not only a unified design but also a regular form of the edge as in Pl. IX, *c*.

A large blanket (Pl. XII, *a*) at the American Museum of Natural History is well designed, but its weaver, instead of allowing freedom for her "over-stuffing" at the edge, "wove it in" with the result that the blanket has a series of diamonds all of which "buckle" or "gather". She wove the diagonal stripes inside; at the ends and edges she used straight weaving with this amusing, or, from my point of view, pathetic result.

The blanket is large, the diamond designs unusually well-spaced, the weaving fine and even. Stretched on the loom it must have looked noble and satisfying. The weaver's chagrin at finding each design element puckered beyond correction when the blanket was taken down can best be realized by one who has had similar disappointments of her own.

Of all the blankets of this type I have seen, a few are good as if made this way consciously; most of them are done in a slovenly manner. Whatever the origin of the style, its technique was never so thoroughly mastered as to become a favorite in Navajo designing.

Clothing

In the old days the woman's dress, or poncho, was woven. It has been frequently described[1] and there is no need to repeat the description here. The weave was usually of the ordinary type, although sometimes borders of diaper pattern, or even of a more complicated raised weave, were used. These ponchos are very rare nowadays, although some of the younger women make reproductions of a later type which are creditable. The oldest poncho was of black, or blue, or both; the later ones of blue, or black and red. I have never seen a reproduction of the oldest kind.

More common is an attempt to weave modern forms of clothing, and certain women have developed great skill in what might be called "woven tailoring". A vest, for instance, of the finest weave, with elaborate and interesting designing, has seams only at the shoulders. This was made with curves at the waist and neck in back and front, so that it fits the owner perfectly. Bullsnake Springs Woman, who made it, has made a number of these vests, learning from each and improving her craftsmanship, especially the shape. Her earlier pieces, excellently finished, had seams under the arms as well as at the shoulders, and her stitching of seams and pockets is so fine as to seem woven. The last vest, woven for Mr. Roman Hubbell, is a great improvement over all the others technically and artistically.

The advance is an original one. The vest was woven widthwise with iron bars, bent to the required curve and size, used as warp-beams. With this loom shaped according to the weaver's requirements, she has been able to finish the vest with the typical Navajo edge and end bindings, even to the revers and the shaped corners at the waist. The specimen is truly remarkable, not only for its originality, but also because of the skill with which the idea has been carried out and the subtle artistry of the designing.

[1] Franciscan Fathers. An Ethnologic Dictionary of the Navaho Language p. 246.
  Matthews, 388.   Amsden, 96.

The designs of ordinary weave, no matter how elaborate they may be when finished, depend solely upon weft regulation. Saddleblanket designs, on the other hand, depend upon the coördination of warp stringing with weft throwing. The variety of results which may be obtained is therefore astonishing, although readily explained by the theory of probabilities.

Blankets of these weaves seem to those of more quiet taste the most artistic of any the Navajo make. They are made primarily for aesthetic and sentimental reasons, since they are almost the only ones the people use themselves. With the exception of the twilled and of the "double-faced" blanket, the technique furnishes such limitations that large expanses of a single color are unusual. No matter what colors are combined, even though they be hard or disagreeable, each shows for such a small space, and is placed so closely to another, that the result of the whole is likely to be soft rather than garish.

Lately the weavers have been executing the saddleblanket weaves in mohair; they combine quietness of color and pattern with softness and fineness of texture. It is interesting and amusing to note that the Navajo man, though acknowledging their artistic superiority, cannot use them because they slide too much. He cannot keep his saddle on his horse if he uses a mohair blanket!

Warp stringing of types A, B, and C (Chap. XII) limit the effects to straight-line designs, but variations may be made by changing colors. Simple plaids are the only possible elaborations of A and B, made by changing the colors of the two alternating weft strands. Not much can be expected in the way of variety when only two rows can be changed. The possibilities are greater for C, where three healds and three wefts may be changed and all their combinations tried.

The diagonal weaves furnish the greatest scope for ideas. Since even the simplest "braided" involves the use of four healds and three weft colors, there may be a large number of effects. It is impossible for me to note *all* the combinations which might occur. I offer a number; others will occur to the worker as understanding of the warp behavior and its relation to the weft becomes more thorough, and as experience develops.

The most common change is in the direction of the diagonal

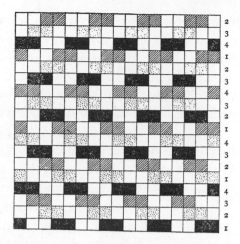

Fig. 27. "Braided", healds reversed, weft not reversed

lines. If the healds are operated in the same succession for the whole distance, the design is of diagonals all running in the same direction; but if, after a time, the order of healds and weft is reversed, the diagonals run in the opposite direction and a herringbone pattern results. These alternations are often continued for the whole surface of the blanket. Pl. VII, *a* shows this effect. If only the healds are reversed and not the wefts, the result will be as in Fig. 27. That is, the herringbone arrangement will be preserved but the colors of the lines will be changed.

A blanket type more common in early days than now is called in trade the "twilled blanket". At first sight it seems no different from the ordinary rug. Upon closer inspection, however, one can readily detect the difference in texture. It is made by stringing the warp as for "braided" (D), and weaving the design as for ordinary weaving. In forming any design of the diagonal weaves the weaver must remember that no row of a pattern is complete unless the four healds have

[*123*]

been thrown. If, for example, any element should be outlined and only two healds are thrown to make the narrowest stripe possible the line will be broken, or have a beaded effect, instead of being continuous as desired. Otherwise there is no additional difficulty. A twilled blanket is slightly thicker than an ordinary one, its texture is desirable, it will withstand harder wear (Pl. X, *c* narrow stripes).

A "twilled" rug which has a design coming to a point in the center may be strung as for a "diamond" whose center is the center warp. With this as the only variation the healds will be strung on either side of it as for "braided", for the principle is the same.

If the twill is strung as "braided", the worker will never reverse the healds but continue for the entire surface in the order in which she began. If it is strung as diamond, she will proceed in order until she comes to the center where she will reverse and continue in that order until the end of the blanket.

Many variations of the "diamond" theme may be suggested. The first and most obvious is the difference in the number of the warps making up the diamond. The lowest is three; there is no limit to the number which may compose it. Because the unit is repeated in close succession, the three-unit pattern has a slightly different effect from those composed of larger units (Pl. VII, *c*). The only restriction is that it must be an odd number. Sometimes, as in the twilled blanket where the design comes to a point in the center, the entire width of the blanket is the unit for the diamond. The Navajo distinguish two diamonds, "small", whose unit may be from three to nine, "large", composed of a unit of eleven or over.

If the healds strung for diamonds are thrown in the same order, 1, 2, 3, 4 continuously, the result is a band of zigzags as in Fig. 22. If they are reversed, a continuous concentric diamond pattern results. Care must be taken to lay the weft colors symmetrically from the point where the change is made. The shape of the diamond depends upon the frequency with which the healds are reversed. If after only

[*124*]

a few rows — they must be multiples of four — the pattern will be low and wide; if there are three is large, the diamond will have all four sides equal.

If the whole is woven in self-color, the cloth has a diaper effect. If only two colors of weft are laid alternately, the diamond effect will be the same but diamonds of only two alternating colors will be concentric. A different effect, such as that of Pl. VIII, *b* may be secured by carrying one color across twice to every one of the first color.

Another plan is to set up the warp for the diamond and to use only three healds for a space, finally using the fourth. This procedure will produce a lozenge as in Pl. X, *b*, which results from a three-unit setup, two weft colors and the use of the healds in the following order: 1, 2, 3, 4, 3, 4, 3, 4, 3, 4, 3, 2, 1.

Pl. VIII, *d* shows a combination warp setup of seven-unit diamond with braided between.

These are a few of the effects which may be attained by variation of warp stringing, order of throwing healds, number of weft colors, and their alternation.

By combining these devices in devious ways the possibilities are almost endless. [Amsden in Pl. 89 shows a beautiful old German-town blanket made by alternating stripes of self-color diamonds (diaper) with stripes of two-color diamonds.] Whereas the deep scallop effect of Pl. X, *d* is secured by using the healds in the order 1, 2, 3, 1, 2, 3, 1, 2, 3, 1, 2, 3, 1, 2, 3, 4, that of Pl. X, *a* is made by the heald order for diamonds until a band is made of the diamond pattern. A wide band succeeds it which consists of vertical stripes of the three colors used until finally heald rod 4 is used again and the order for diamonds is repeated.

Such blankets having simple variations or alternations of the diagonal weaves are usually more restful to the eye than those on which a single pattern is repeated monotonously over the whole surface. Another satisfactory mode is to intercept three-color braided or diamond by bands of self-color twill or diaper. An interesting stripe arrangement is shown in Pl. X, *c* where wide two-color braided bands are broken up by narrower bands woven of two colors, one the same, one different from those used in the wide bands, set in as if weft in ordinary weaving.

If only two colors of weft are alternated with a braided warp setup, the result is a fine wavy pattern. The reason this does not happen in Pl. X, *c* is that the dark color is carried across two sheds to the white's one; in other words, the arrangement is not a simple alternation.

A peculiar arrangement of broken diamonds is shown in Pl. XI, *c*, the count for which is Pl. XI, *d*.

Designing Double-faced Cloth

In discussing the technique of double-faced cloth (Chap. XII). I described one of the easiest setups for this peculiar fabric. As is the case with the diagonal weaves, the possible combination of patterns is without limit. On the basis of the simple blanket set up for me by Juan's-Wife and of the explanations given me by Mrs. Nanaba Bryan, I have worked out the principle of the double-faced cloth which I shall explain before I take up the specific patterns worked out from it. An understanding of this theory will enable the weaver to work out any designs she wishes for any type of double-faced cloth she may see fit to attempt.

The explanation is as follows: After deciding on the pattern she wishes to use for face and reverse, the weaver knows how she would count the warps for each if it were separate. In the case in point (Fig. 23), ordinary weave (face) means that she must have certain warps on one heald, the alternating ones on the other, one over, one

PLATE XI

[a]
Double-faced blanket, same design
on both sides (courtesy Lloyd
Ambrose)

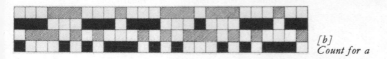

[b]
Count for a

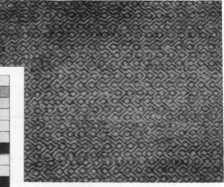

[c]
Broken diamond

[d]
Count for c

PLATE XII

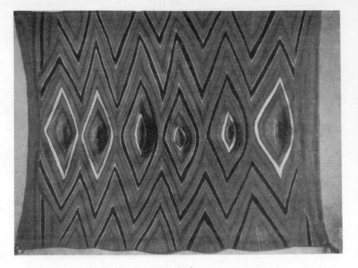

[a]
Blanket with mismanaged "overstuffing"
(courtesy American Museum of Natural History)

[c]
Count for b

[b]
Large double-faced blanket
(courtesy B. I. Staples)

under quite simply. For "speckled" (reverse) she must have two up and two down all the way across the blanket, that is, certain pairs on one heald and the alternating pairs on the other.

Every time a shed is made for the double-faced cloth the heald must pull forward, not only the alternating warps for its own design, but also some belonging to the reverse pattern. For example, if I pull forward heald 1, I want to throw my weft so that one strand is up and the next one down, but at the same time I must prevent this weft from showing on the opposite side. Shed 1, therefore, has three warps forward for every one it really needs. Shed 2 must do the same, and, although the weft will show only as lying over strands 2, 6, 10, 14, etc., the heald will be pulling three strands (Nos. 3, 4, 5; 7, 8, 9; 11, 12, 13, etc.) forward.

The healds 3 and 4 will need two strands alternating in pairs each time they are thrown, for the white and brown wefts will show at the back always in spaces of two warps. Nevertheless, the healds raise three of the warp strands every time they need only two. That is, each heald must not only get its own opposites out of the way but it must also keep one of the strands regulating the face pattern forward.

In fixing the sheds one must always see to it that healds 3 and 4 pull forward one more strand than is necessary for the design at the back, and that healds 1 and 2 leave one more back in the same way. Thus, if a pattern requires combinations of two strands, the heald must regulate three; if it needs only one, the heald must pull forward two.

Let us take another example, this one if possible even simpler than the first. There will be ordinary weave on both sides. It matters not what the design will be, as long as it is ordinary weave, design will have nothing to do with the warp count. If face and reverse were each separate, we should want one warp up, one down. Since we have to reckon one more than the required number for one shed, we shall loop the healds as in Pl. XII, c.

A careful study of the counts for the double-faced blanket shows that in two rows (the ones which make the face design), the weft is caught under only one warp and shows for a number larger than one (in Fig. 23 for three, and in Pl. XII, *c* for two). For the opposite two rows, the colors which are to make the reverse pattern are forward on only one, which means that the weft shows on the opposite side for a space of at least two warps or more. Usually the weaver uses a heavier yarn for the face design than for the reverse. As she weaves, she notices that the weft which forms the design at the back lies lower than that which forms the design on the face. The catching of the weft for either side by only one warp on the opposite side allows it to be hidden, but at the same time furnishes a guide, a kind of dim pattern, to the weaver.

[This is the explanation of Mr. Amsden's puzzle (Navaho Weaving, p. 59), about which I cannot forbear to remark: "It would be difficult to work a figured pattern into the back of a two-faced blanket, merely because the weaver cannot see that part of her fabric, hence would have great difficulty in placing the weft colors in their proper arrangement for pattern building. She might conceivably carry the back pattern in her head and work from a mental picture of its exact layout, spacing, and progress toward completion; but to do so would be a mental feat fully equal to that of the chess expert playing several games at once." I pause here to note that almost any Navajo rug with elaborate and detailed design is a feat much greater than the one here suggested. Since compositions are "carried in her head" by a Navajo weaver and since she always "works from a mental picture of the layout", it does not seem to me incredible that some weavers achieve just this thing. Expert typists do not look at the results of their work as they are doing it, pianists do not watch their keys, why does an expert weaver need more than a simple guide to the design on the back of her weaving? This she has in the form of the weft from the back which shows through. The weaving of two designs does not seem miraculous to me judging only from my own experience with weaving the double-faced. I even go so far as to say that I, who hold myself for the veriest amateur, could design and execute such a blanket.]

[To continue with Mr. Amsden's speculations: "Two weavers, one building the back pattern only and the other weaving the front and manipulating heddles and batten could produce an astonishing double pattern. One weaver alone could scarcely handle the two patterns without rising from her seat and going around the loom to look at the back pattern at almost every shift of the heddle — unless she used a large mirror back of the loom."

I hope Mr. Amsden had his tongue in his cheek when he wrote that scene. The most apparent remark a Navajo could make to it would be "who but a white man would think of *that*?"]

The setup for the huge blanket of Pl. XII, *b* was that of Pl. XII, *c*. This famous rug is typical, too, of the most common arrangement of designs on the two sides: a pattern of ordinary weave, it matters not how elaborate, on the face, a striped design on the back. Motives other than stripes may be used on the two sides of the same blanket (Pl. VI, *d*), showing that it is possible to make a design even though it cannot be seen by the weaver. It is, however, far more expedient to use for the reverse a pattern which can be achieved by throwing the shuttle reed all the way across the rug.

Pl. XI, *a* shows a variation of the double-faced cloth. The difference between this and the other examples given is that where they have different designs on front and back, this one has the same design, and that a simple one, on both sides. That is, the colors are the same and cover spaces of the same size but they are opposite each other; if the block is red on face, it is white on reverse and so on.

[Mr. Amsden puts this type of blanket into a class by itself calling it "doublecloth", voicing his doubt that it is Navajo, although its internal evidence convinces him (only one of the many examples in

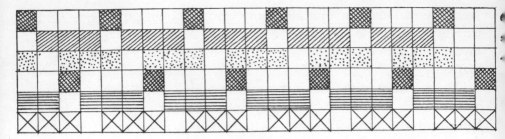

Fig. 28. Count for double-faced: Braided on face, ordinary on reverse

his book, by the way, that he appreciates evidence and weighs it carefully), and resorting to an explanation of it from Peruvian material. I am sure both Mr. Amsden and Mr. Schweizer, who lent him the piece, will be gratified to know it is one hundred percent Navajo on the basis of evidence which I secured quite naïvely. Maria Antonia had a modern blanket similar to the one Mr. Amsden figures in his Pl. 33, *d*, which she told me her sister wove. I did not take the counts of this blanket but I know the weaving was exactly the same as that of Pl. XI, *a*, although it was much finer.

The woman who taught me to weave the belt had the blanket whose counts are given in Pl. XI, *b* set up on her loom and about a quarter finished. Della, my interpreter, wanted to make one like it and we took down the counts. It follows in every particular of setup and manipulation the rules for weaving double-faced (Amsden calls it "two-faced") cloth.]

Fig. 28 is a rig I set up for myself as a kind of freak blanket, but by no means inconceivable. The count is for braided on the face and ordinary weave on the reverse. The reason it is more complicated than any I have considered is that it involves six healds. I have tried it out on my loom and the conception and counts are accurate.

A saddleblanket brought to the Gallup Ceremonial in 1935 had a diamond pattern on one side and braided on the other. Its maker told the trader to whom she brought it that she had used six healds but I believe it would require eight.

Lightning Designs

No phase of nature or of culture lends itself to strict classification into rigid categories and Navajo blankets are no exception. The classes into which technical procedures and designs fall are not numerous. Nevertheless, there are a few styles of rug which cut across the boundaries of several. One of those is the twilled rug which is strung as braided and woven like the ordinary weave. Another is the so-called "lightning" rug. It is the design made by bands formed of diagonal lines and variously arranged. It is not a favorite with the Navajo now; in fact, I have never seen a modern specimen of this kind. There are three ways of making it. The first is, as I explained Maria Antonia worked it out (p. 96), by inserting narrow portions of weft all the way across the rug so as to build up the design by ordinary weaving. If this method were used, the rug would have a straight edge.

The most commonly known pattern of this sort is made in the scalloped-edge style, a method of treatment most suitable to it. I think it not at all unlikely that the scalloped edge was an outgrowth of the diagonal laying of the weft, accidental perhaps at first, and later striven for. James[1] in his Fig. 145 shows one of the more slovenly ones. This one is almost certainly a twilled blanket. The unevenness of the edge is due to poor workmanship rather than a different technical process. Whatever the weaver of this blanket aimed for, she achieved little consistency. Fig. 144[1] is one of the best of these blankets I have ever seen; [Pl. 24 in Amsden (Navaho Weaving) shows two others better done than usual].

[1] Indian Blankets and their Makers.

[The design of Amsden Pl. 25 is of the lightning category but it has straight edges. I can account for this fact in two ways. One explanation is that, since the diagonal stripes were carried past the middle from each side, the weft was introduced evenly and had no reason to bulge at the edge. The other, and that a more plausible one, is that the blanket is twilled; I cannot tell from the illustration.]

A third way of securing the lightning pattern is by twilling, a medium admirably suited to the purpose. The warp is rigged for braided; the weft is introduced as in the ordinary weave; the resulting blanket has a straight edge (James, Fig. 143; [Amsden, Pl. 25(?)]). In weaving the "lightning" as well as any other design by twilling it must be remembered that no "row" is complete unless all four healds have been used; that is, the design will be perfected only after the weft has been carried through four sheds.

XV Warp Weaving

Besides blankets and rugs of varied styles and techniques, the Navajo make a number of objects, belts, sashes, garters, and headbands, in a technique which relies for effect on principles entirely different from those already discussed. In this weave, the warp only is seen, the weft being covered completely. Although warp weaving is frequently seen among the Navajo, there is nothing about it which is distinctively Navajo. Indeed, it is often impossible to tell a Navajo belt from a Hopi one. Occasionally the colors are different but they are not typically so. Navajo belts are most often made of red and green Germantown warp with the weft of white cord, which serves also for warp decoration and edges. Hopi belts generally have black and more green than the Navajo, but some of red, black, and white appear identical in style.

It is likely that the Hopi employ some differences in motor habits, but they are so slight as to be indiscernible in the finished product. Furthermore, there is nothing except the peculiarity of design and the fact it is handmade to distinguish it from a white man's product. No native materials are used.

The warp-weaver secures a ball of thin white cord of the variety commonly used by grocers, and several skeins of Germantown yarn, scarlet and green in color. Rarely is a Navajo satisfied with yarn as she buys it and in warp weaving she is no exception. The Germantown of commerce is a four-ply, somewhat loosely twisted yarn. Using the short end of her spindle as described for twisting plies in Lessons 3—5 (Pl. III, c), she transforms the soft Germantown into a harder, finer, tightly twisted filament.

If she is making a belt, she has in mind the length and width, and proceeds to construct her loom accordingly. The essential difference between this loom and the ordinary one is that it takes care of the entire length of the object to be woven, so that the warp is stretched continuously over two rounded sticks (cp. Pl. IV, *d* for old style handling of warp in similar way). The loom consists simply of two long poles, preferably with protuberances to which the strings tying the cross-poles may be firmly tied. Pl. XIII, *a* shows the setup of the loom before the warp wrapping. There is nothing complicated about it; its chief requirement is strength. It must be firm enough not to move at all during the entire process of weaving. The upper cross-stick may be permanently tied to the uprights, but the lower one must be adjustable, for only by pressing down on this is there any means of tightening the warp.

The belt here described is seven feet long with fringe twelve inches long at each end. That means the loom had to accommodate warp nine feet two inches long, for the fringe is a part of the warp. Since it was double, the distance between the cross-poles was four feet eight inches. This was too long for one woman to reach with control of the yarn and two women strung the warp; one standing, carried the ball over the upper cross-pole, the other sitting, carefully regulated the position of every strand in its particular relation to the others. This was a permanent adjustment of warp, not a temporary one such as was made for the rug or blanket. The stringing was similar to that made on the warpframe (cp. p. 53) except that the threads were not made to cross between the poles.

Since the warp is the design-element, it is carefully counted as it is wrapped into place, and each wrapping is arranged and counted in pairs (the figures below indicate *pairs* of warp of each color):

wh	red	gr	red	gr	red	wh
2	10	10	55	10	10	2

The warp-stringing is begun at the bottom by tying a loop over the lower cross-pole, and it is finished with a loop of the same kind tied over the upper cross-pole diagonally opposite. The finished belt is five inches wide, but there was no evidence of its ultimate width during the stringing, for the warps stood far apart, as may be seen in Pl. XIII, *b*. After the red and green pairs had been satisfactorily adjusted, the white cords were strung, two pairs on each side to serve as a border and thirty-five pairs in the center to help form the design, for pattern is confined to the center in this kind of weaving.

The warp is laid firmly enough to lie nicely in place, but it is not tight. The reason it should not be tight is because of the next adjustment. A round stick is looped into every other pair of strands as in Fig. 29; that is, those pairs which later lie over the heald rod.[1] Another round stick takes up in the same way the alternate pairs, those which are looped into the harness. These two round sticks may be rolled up or down the warp and serve the purpose of keeping the warps separated on the under side. If they are not used, it is difficult to separate the sheds because the strands of Germantown cling together.

The weaver then arranges her sheds as she would for ordinary weave. Alternate pairs of warp are laid over the heald rod; the others looped as usual except that an extra loop is inserted between each pair of warps. Since these warps are in pairs, there is a larger space between them, and the second loop holds the setup firmly.

The belt is now ready for weaving. An amount of white cord is wound on a stick so that it may easily be inserted as a shuttle. A small, smooth, flat stick slightly wider than the belt is at hand. Instead of a comb, a stubby, rather heavy

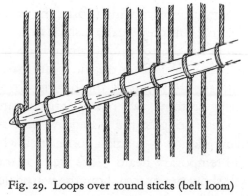

[1] The illustration shows only one strand taken over the round stick and one left under, but there should be a pair in each position.

Fig. 29. Loops over round sticks (belt loom)

club is used to beat down the weft. From this point on, such efficiency as the weaver has developed through habit in ordinary weaving will be a hindrance rather than a help, for the club is used instead of the comb and batten. The weaver has learned, after discouraging experience, to keep her weaving from tightening; now she can hardly pull the weft-cord tight enough.

She will throw a heald so as to make a shed, insert the stick-shuttle which carries the cord, and then she will reduce the width of the warp to about half by pulling the weft-cord in so tight that it does not show under the warp. At the same time she must be very careful not to break the weft because this cord has little strength. Still another reason for pulling it as tight as its strength allows is to make a nice edge. If the tension is just right, the turn of the weft makes a neat twist with the white edge-warps and all seem to be combined in a single regular unit.

When the weaver has made a row by manipulating the healds exactly as she would for ordinary weaving, but drawing the thin weft-cord so tight that it is covered by the heavier weft, and pounding it home with the club, she will have a row of stitches like the widest white ones of Pl. XIII, c. The club serves to separate the sheds and to pound the weft down to the lower cross-pole. The belt moves automatically down and back around the pole every time a row is set in.

Now the rows which form the white background make a kind of design, but they really establish a contrasting background in the center for the red and green of the sides. The actual pattern of these belts is a design set on the white background which is made by the ordinary throwing of the healds. In this case, there were two alternating patterns, two rows of zigzags and a queue. Before starting one of these designs, the Navajo weaver makes two rows using her last manipulation — a small, loose stick which acts as a kind of subsidiary and temporary heald. It is well for the learner to try this, too, for it will show her exactly how the warps lie when they are so handled.

She raises the heald on which the white threads lie, runs the sword through the shed. Then, on the small stick she picks up the red warps of the center and holds them up with her left hand while she passes the weft through the shed with her right. She operates the second heald exactly as usual and throws the weft across twice more as usual. The effect of this operation is to make a row of red which looks like the solid dark part between the patterns on the horizontal portion of Pl. XIII, c. The belt is photographed so as to show both sides, one of which is the reverse of the other.

The explanation of this is as follows: The warp of the center, if manipulated in the usual fashion lies in alternate colors, red on one heald, white on the other. If, however, on one row across, which would ordinarily be white, the red warps of the center are taken up, there will be a red pattern on the white two warp-rows wide. That is all there is to making the belt designs. If a design is to be made, the red warps which compose it will be taken up wherever necessary to form it. Correspondingly, the reverse will have a white pattern in exactly the same place as the red on the face. The entire belt appears as if having a central panel with a raised design. It will be noticed that the stitches of the border and of the center are the same, the difference in appearance being due to the presence of white in the center, except of course where the design exists in the center. There, it seems raised because each warp composing it extends over three wefts whereas the others cover only one.

When this manipulation is understood, the weaver can make any design she wishes within the limitations of her space which are reasonably narrow. Two central patterns are given in Figs. 30, 31, reading warp now instead of weft as over or under. Other patterns can readily be worked out. If the design is one which is symmetrical from the center, as is Fig. 31, an extra row (weft through two sheds) is made for the center-design which is not made for the border. For that center row, manipulated in the manner described, the red design

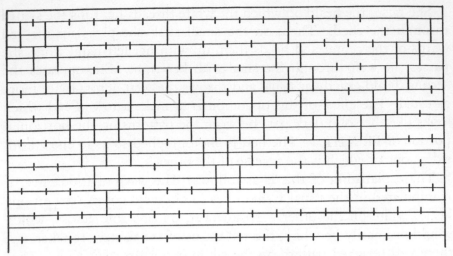

Fig. 30. Warp count for zigzag pattern

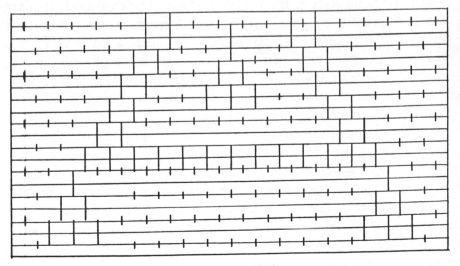

Fig. 31. Warp count for half of queue pattern

warps lie over four instead of three wefts and from there the design is made in reverse.

The description of the loom and the belt illustrated is that of the largest and most elaborate type of fabric in warp weaving. Like special types of rugs, belts are woven in particular regions. When as wide as this one, they are used as maternity belts to furnish support. Shorter, narrower strips for headbands, hatbands or garters may be set up in the same way on a portable loom, like that of Pl. XIII, *d* made of a fork of a tree. Sometimes the upper end of the warp is put over a rigid pole or rod, and the lower end fastened to the belt or about the waist of the weaver. These are merely different methods of stretching the warp; all other features of the weaving are the same.

Errors in warp weaving are noticeable even to the inexperienced eye. Even if the weaver detects a mistake just a row after it has been made, she finds it difficult to ravel for the warp is tight, strong, and firmly interwoven with the thin, easily-broken cord. It can be done, of course, but the careful weaver avoids mistakes even more carefully than in tapestry weaving where they are less noticeable and more easily corrected. That was the reason Della's Grandmother, who showed me how to make the belt, did not wish to have me work on it, and allowed me to make only two of the designs, anxiously prompting me on the counts, even insisting on taking over the weaving when she thought a mistake was imminent. Consequently, I did not really understand the principles involved until I had cut a forked branch and set up my own loom, when the errors, as always, taught me as much as the correct weaving.

After the weaving has been carried on for the length of the garter, band, or belt until only six to fifteen inches are left unfinished, the weaver ties the last row of her cord-weft so it cannot slip. She then cuts the warp at half the distance remaining unwoven. The band falls from the loom with unruly warp strands at each end. The weaver patiently separates them into groups of four or five strands each and twists these groups as if to make one string, thus making a neat fringe. Although the fringe may seem decorative to White eyes, it is more than that to the Indian who uses it to fasten her belt. Once she has the belt wrapped about her waist, perhaps twice, she tucks the fringe in and thus keeps her belt firmly in place.

The only exact description I know of this weaving is the short article by Leslie Spier on Zuñi Weaving Technique[1], which describes the technique of the Navajo exactly.

I have already noted that, although there may be categories of style and of techniques, at the same time there is overlapping. An example of that for warp and weft weaving is the saddle-cinch. The warp is looped through the rings of the cinch as if they were the loom beams. One is then attached to some firm object, such as a pole or a branch, and the other may be tied to the weaver's belt. The setup of the loom is that of warp weaving, but the weaving itself is done on a saddleblanket weave, usually diamond or "braided" with four healds.

[1] American Anthropologist 26 (1900): 74—76.

PLATE XIII

[a]
Belt loom before warp
is strung

[b]
Belt loom with warp
nearly strung

[c]
Detail of belt showing both sides

[e]
Detail of d

[d]
Loom for small band

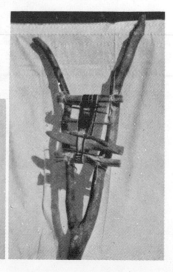

PLATE XIV

[a]
Detail of old design

[b]
Detail ol allover design
in many colors

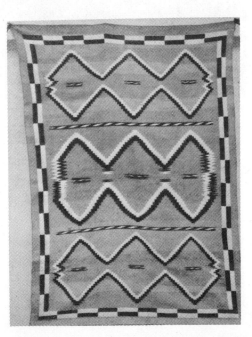

[c]
Comb pattern

[d]
Blanket illustrated by James, Fig. 13
(courtesy Metropolitan Museum)

XVI *Style*

A well-known ethnologist once remarked that someone ought to make a study of the style of Navajo blankets. A student answered, "But how could anyone? The style doesn't stay put long enough." The remark is as true as it is flippant. Navajo rugs have a style of their own, a character which so distinguishes them that, with rare exceptions, one can be picked out of hundreds in a collection from the world. The exception might be old Hopi or, perchance, a few Mexican blankets.

The general characteristics are coarseness and crudeness of material and weave, barbaric or very quiet colors, often a combination of both, designs on face and back similar, with the same, not alternating colors, and use of the simplest design-elements. Materials and technique remain incredibly stable, designs change overnight. It is impossible to indicate all the variations in style but certain tendencies may be pointed out.

Although he has no direct contact with the manufacturer, the taste of the white consumer dictates what the trader, who is the middleman, may accept and what he must reject. The trader, then, is the one who judges, criticises, makes suggestions, delivers the final decree which registers on his cash register or daybook. Actually the trader (those I know at least) rarely rejects. No matter how bad a blanket is, even technically, he shakes his head, says dubiously, "It is not good," but offers something at least for it. But, like a teacher or a mother, he says also, "You must do better next time." If the woman is not satisfied, thinks his scolding unjust, she may peddle the blanket about, offering it to other traders. If it is really bad, she gets little for it and will mend her ways.

Luckily for the Navajo and for the art, every trader has a clientèle whose tastes are versatile, and, what is more, the caprice of each group of followers differs greatly, so that each trading post is really somewhat representative for its locality. There are stories of the way blankets change hands as entertaining as tales of horse trading. A trader has an expensive blanket with no ostensible faults. He simply cannot sell it. He trades it for another, perhaps less expensive and less artistic. The chances are that both traders will sell the rugs to their mutual advantage. The business is an uncertain one, but there are many styles that take.

Where do the Navajo get their designs? Since the beginning of weaving, the time of which we do not know, they have had a few simple designs. The most common are obtuse and acute-angled triangles which if doubled form rectangles or parallelograms; stripes, horizontal, vertical and diagonal. As I have already pointed out (Chap. XI), all the patterns of ordinary weaving are based on these elements.

Composition is determined by an infinite number of factors. The earliest stock-in-trade of arrangements may be briefly placed in three classes, the most common of which is the division of the surface into bands (center of Pl. XIV, d). Often the bands consist of a group of stripes, placed at top and bottom, and a wide, more highly elaborated band at the center. Sometimes the bands are all the same size and arranged at regular intervals from top to bottom. A second type might be called an allover design. A large diamond pattern, often with terraced boundary, may be repeated regularly over the surface (Pl. XIV, a). There is usually a small simple design within the diamond.

A third class of arrangement, not common, but always well carried out, shows the influence of the Chimayo blanket. In this type the entire surface may be composed of small triangles or parallelograms of many colors (Pl. XIV, b). The triangles frequently form a compact, sometimes disturbing, continuity of pattern. In other cases, the blanket has a background, and zigzags, diamonds, or diagonal stripes are arranged so that the background breaks up the closely decorated surface and sets it off.

Many of the blankets of these three types look elaborate, but analysis shows their fundamental simplicity. Those in the style of the first and second types do not commonly have a large number of colors. A background of bright red, or the rose-red of bayeta, with designs carried out in two or three contrasting colors, white, indigo blue, and perhaps pale green, is a typical combination. Outstanding designs made up of groups of stripes often have blue or white backgrounds as well as red.

By definition, the third style was composed of a large number of colors, all, it seems, a given weaver could acquire. She did not need much yarn of the same color to make a single one of the figures. Often she laid in a triangle or parallelogram of a color and never repeated it. Indeed there are cases where her color did not suffice to finish even one simple small figure. For example, the base half of a triangle may be light green and the figure finished in yellow. There is no reason to suppose that the weaver did not know how to match her colors; it is more likely she lacked the one she needed. There were undoubtedly in the old days, even as now, those workers to whom matching made no difference, but there were also those who had a remarkable feeling for balance, even for symmetry. These wove blankets carefully calculated as to color. If there is a light green triangle in the upper left hand corner, there is one to balance it in the lower right, or even in each corner.

A variant of the striped ornamentation is the so-called "chief" blanket (Pls. VI, c; XV, c). This has a striped background; in the older ones it was blue and black, or blue and white, or blue, white, and black. In the center there may be a large complete diamond with terraced bounding sides, and at each corner a quarter of the same diamond pattern, so arranged that if corners of the blanket are folded in to the center they form a diamond which coincides exactly with that at the center. The "chief" blankets have characteristic proportions, one and one-eighth to one and one-half times as wide as long.

The stripes of the background run horizontally. This blanket, worn by men in early times, is the one which has been replaced by the modern "Pendleton" of machine manufacture now worn by all adult Navajo on special occasions.

Within the last few years there has been a revival of the chief blanket. In some localities several of them may be seen in a blanket-room at one time. Practically all I have seen are well designed and well woven. Discriminating Whites like them and the future for them seems good. They are usually made of the more quiet colors, but the contrast of the diamonds with the background makes them admirably showy. There is a constant tendency for the design to occupy more space, a development in harmony with the general elaboration of style in modern times [cp. Amsden, Pls. 74, 75, 90, 91a, 98].

Stylistically the closest relative of the old blanket with stripe ornamentation is the modern "vegetable dye" blanket, made principally in the vicinity of Fort Defiance, Chinlee, and as far west and north as the Black Mountain region.

The designs used in this kind of soft cover are usually of the simplest stripes or elements, combined in bands. The commonest background is white. The designs are carried out in various shades of brown, green, yellow, and rose. Some browns are muddy and dull as compared with certain clear browns, russets and tans, some of which are the natural colors of the wool of some sheep. The greens are all yellowish; I have rarely seen a blue green in contemporary natural dyes. The yellows are pale but soft, with great variety of shades and tones.

The overwhelming tendency at the present time is to make blankets unified by a border. This bias has had its effect on the "vegetable dye" blanket also, although it has not yet reached its limit.

One (Pl. XV, *a*) which is large as these blankets come, six feet wide by six and one-half feet long, has the sand background and relative sparsity of design in common with the old style. But it shows the modern tendency in its border, set in from the edge, it is true, but nevertheless a unifying arrangement. This border is quite complex, being a large zigzag composed of a white center stripe with wide black and narrow yellow on each side. The four center designs, parallelograms composed of white, black, and gray with pale yellow outline, are old-fashioned components. The result is harmonious, well balanced, well spaced, satisfactory.

Another modern rug of natural colors has a daring combination of rose, dark yellow and gray arranged in wide terraced diagonals; the combination repeated symmetrically from the center makes a continuous unified decoration. This blanket has only the colors and elements of old blankets; the composition is ultra-modern and of the best. It is striking, unique, and completely satisfying.

I have decribed the two vegetable dye blankets in detail to show how their revival is influenced by style in ordinary modern blankets. The description shows also that the chief fault of the common rug is gaudiness of color and perhaps over-exuberance of design, although the latter need not be a fault.

Whereas the relationship of the vegetable dye blankets to their aged predecessors may be readily seen — they may in fact be considered a continuous development — there is another style of modern blanket whose close stylistic kinship can hardly be detected. The Navajo women make small blankets and cushion-tops which have primarily the designs used in the old blankets of many colors, composed of small triangles and parallelograms. The traders may furnish Germantown yarns for these, having them made to order, or the Navajo, in rare cases, buy the Germantowns.

In spite of the fact that the articles made of them are technically almost perfect, they are popular only with the most inexperienced of buyers. Even the traders I know who carry them in stock do not really try to sell them. I have looked over piles and piles of blankets. In more than one case I have been told in answer to a question, "And what are these?" "Those? Oh! those are just Germantowns." An exception to this is the attempt at reproducing old blankets in Germantown. I feel, however, that the criticism of the next paragraph is justified even for these.

The reason for the attitude of traders and the relative unpopularity with buyers is, I suspect, the fact that the Germantowns have no character. The dominating colors are dark or gay; often, each color, taken by itself, is lovely. But the combination of colors results in something which is neither White because it is hand-woven, nor is it Navajo because the yarn is machine-made and chemically dyed. More than anything they resemble Mexican rugs, but somehow the style does not ring true.

The relationship between modern patterns and their earlier relatives is a remote one, although fundamental. More usually the designs are unique, their weavers' minds being so versatile that it is seldom possible to determine from what source or sources they drew their inspiration. They are subjected to a great many influences, indeed, and as they are "rug-minded" as well as "sheep-minded", they look for suggestions on every scrap of paper.

My family was intensely interested in the patterns of James' *"Indian Blankets and their Makers"* — so interested that they had a friend copy several of them.

James describes the blanket of Pl. XIV, *d* as a "valuable old bayeta". My Navajo friends criticised it roundly because the illustration as they saw it showed mishandling of the design. The blanket is woven of red, blue and white; in James' illustration the difference between blue and red did not come out, so that it seemed as if the white zigzags were miscalculated. Pl. XIV, *d* is a new photograph of this blanket which shows why James praised it so highly. It shows by the shading how interestingly the weaver divided her working spaces. The border is interesting also, for it is a good example of "border within border".

One day, when I was using *An Ethnologic Dictionary of the Navaho*

Language by the Franciscan Fathers, Atlnaba took it out of my hands to scrutinize the symbol of the Franciscan order on the fly-leaf which she said would make a good rug pattern. I have not seen all the rugs these women wove during the winter, so that I do not know whether they used the designs or not. If they have not used them yet, it does not mean that they never will.

The name, J. L. Hubbell, is cast in the iron entrance gate of his homestead. A woman wove a huge rug, well done in every way and at the bottom she had woven J. L. Hubbell with the L turned backward. Mr. Hubbell had not ordered it; he did not want it, but he felt himself obliged to buy it, though of course he could never sell it.

At another place on the Reservation a woman, upon every visit to the trading post, boasted of the fine blanket she was making. It also was large and took a long time to weave; besides, the trader knew she was an excellent weaver. Her pride was so great that after a time the trader's curiosity was considerably aroused and he awaited the rug with great expectations. What was his surprise, therefore, when his client finally unrolled her *chef d'oeuvre* from the folds of a capacious floursack, to see slowly but surely emerge a complete imitation of the Ivory soap wrapper, letters and all. He was more fortunate than Mr. Hubbell for the manufacturers of Ivory Soap bought it from him.

Every trader can tell of experiences of the sort, some with a happy, others with a more disappointing, ending. The tragedy is usually for the trader, for a Navajo woman cannot see why letters on a rug should make it worthless. She sees the letters as design. Of course the number of rugs with a complete facsimile of a trade wrapper is relatively small. Large, however, is the number having designs taken from wrappers of coffee, cereal, bread, candy. The simpler geometric designs are copied most often, but there are many craftswomen who undertake the most elaborate designs and, what is more, carry them out successfully.

Whether or not the influence came primarily from the package goods wrapper, Navajo rugs of the present day are decorated according to principles of composition quite different from those of an earlier day. Most characteristically the surface is seen as a whole surrounded by a border. The use of the border shows a change in Navajo psychology because there used to be a belief, still felt by the devout, that a worker "should not weave herself in". The ceremonial basket, still used extensively, but not often made by the Navajo, with its "trail" to let the spirit out, illustrates the feeling. The numerous and beautiful sandpaintings which embody the real symbolism of the Navajo usually have some bounding element, a rainbow garland, a chain of arrows, or a snake, but such elongated elements are never closed. There is an opening at the east or the northeast.

When an emotion like this, strongly rooted in religion, can be changed by the growing importance of the material life, it seems as if almost any new idea might be taken over. The means by which the fear of weaving oneself in has weakened were gradual and natural. No trader thought, when he stowed a package of oatmeal on his shelves, that he would be an unconscious influence on the style of Navajo weaving. The frequent imitation of designs copied from trade goods and their economic success has worn down the Navajo objection to such an extent that a great many rugs are woven according to the new principles and not even a thread is left for a "path". Maria Antonia and her daughters are as orthodox as any Navajo in many respects. I have seen numerous rugs of their weaving, all with unbroken borders.

But when Atlnaba weaves a sandpainting, she naturally weaves the conventional rainbow or enclosing symbol because that is a part of the picture she is copying; it will not be a continuous symbol. She also weaves a border to the blanket; those I have seen are black against the "sheep gray" background. And in order to "be on the safe side" she carries a gray strand through her border for one row. Sandpaintings possess "power", if used properly, for good; if abused, they may

[148]

turn evil against the one who handles them. The weaving of sand-paintings is a "misuse of power", and therefore dangerous. One can readily understand then why Atlnaba in making this kind of composition relapses to the old custom.

The most modern innovation, then, is the border arrangement. Within the now unified surface a great many variations are apparent. Some borders are straight and smooth, others have broken lines inside, many of them are dark, black predominates, some are of the background color, giving an effect of a border carried in from the edge.

At Ganado, where I learned weaving, there are several outstanding characteristics of the many blankets which come to the J. L. Hubbell Trading Post. That most noticeable is the use of red backgrounds with black borders, another is the frequency of the "comb" design (Pl. XIV, c). Many customers like red backgrounds; they sell better than dull ones. I have never seen better demonstration of virtuosity than in some of these rugs.

When a worker has his craft under control he may "play with the technique" in various ways to demonstrate his skill. This may be done in several ways. Fineness may be reduced to smallness. A man carves the Lord's Prayer on the head of a pin, a Pomo Indian basket-maker fashions a basket so small it must be kept in a tiny bottle. Vastness is another expression of highly developed skill. The women weave, they weave well, they will prove it by weaving the largest rugs they can. The complications which arise in laying out and executing these rugs are legion. The amount of warp they require is almost immeasurable, to mention only one item. All the women at Hastin Gani's spun for a year to prepare the yarn for the sandpainting tapestry his wife wove in a month. She had to have poles sixteen feet long. She needed a special place to weave and her loom extended above the roof of her weaving shed.

An expert may show her supremacy by exaggerating size or by providing herself with complications. The most skilful Navajo weaver does both, for with gigantism goes design elaboration. As is to be expected, the rule is that the larger the blanket attempted the more pretentious the design and the smaller the number of errors.

Another feature of large and small rugs in the vicinity I know best is the fondness for combining red with yellow or orange. A rug fourteen feet square has a red background with black border, and the design, composed of fine lines well-spaced and regular, is black, white and yellow. Mr. Hubbell has had also a number of sandpaintings woven on a red background. They always have much yellow, blue, black, and white.

Besides red-background, bordered, and accurate sandpainting rugs, all large, the J. L. Hubbell Trading Post is encouraging the mohair blanket. I have seen perhaps half a dozen of these altogether; four were brought to this post, one I bought directly from the loom of Maria Antonia; all are beyond criticism. It may be that in the days when cash is scarce, the development will be retarded. Or the fact that higher prices are paid for mohair may militate against a speedy increase in the number of the rugs. The third drawback is the difficulty with which the mohair is spun. It is too early to predict the course of this interesting expansion. The goat, in spite of much ranger pressure against it, has a secure place in the Navajo heart. It may be that its hair will usurp the place of wool in the weaver's workbox. I think it more likely that it will be used only by those few who have an aesthetic, as well as an economic interest in their craft. If that is the case, it will occupy a place of honor among the thousands of rugs pounded out on the Navajo loom.[1]

In contrast to the crimson backgrounds of the rugs made at Ganado are the famous "Two-Gray-Hills" rugs, made in the region east of the Chuskai Mountains (Pl. XV, *b*). They rarely have red in them; if

---

[1] This opinion was written before the "goat-hunting" campaign of the U. S. Government began in 1933. At the moment (1936) it seems likely that the mohair blanket will become a rare piece.

PLATE XV

[d]
Modern realistic designs
(courtesy Linda Musser)

[e]
Modern realistic designs
(courtesy Linda Musser)

[a]
Vegetable dye blanket with border

[c]
Chief blanket [courtesy Lloyd Ambrose])

[b]
Two-Gray-Hills blanket (courtesy
A. J. Newcomb)

it occurs, it is in small quantity. They are usually medium-sized — they may be reasonably large, but are never gigantic — bordered compositions of white, gray, black, and brown. The designs are varied, indeed, but the composition is characterized by the fact that many small elements are woven in, and the arrangement of the design units is balanced or symmetrical. The weavers of these blankets do not exploit the background. Ordinarily they leave little space unfilled with design. On the other hand, they make elaborate borders, one within another. The rugs often give the appearance of two or three rugs of graduated sizes, neatly and regularly placed one on top of the other. The Two-Gray-Hills rugs have long enjoyed great fame. They are liked for the modesty and good combination of colors and for the perfection of their technique. They are woven of yarn, as evenly and finely spun as any the Navajo make except perhaps the mohair.

Pl. XV, *a*, detail of an old blanket, illustrates many points of Navajo style, all typical, as is the whole blanket. It shows also the difficulty in classifying design and composition. The rhombus with toothed edges, composed of small triangles, is an old and favorite arrangement. This blanket has a background also, but it is broken up into many diagonal bands formed by serrations which are "outlined". The blanket has three borders at the sides, the edges of all arranged in the "comb" pattern. It might be called a "blanket with allover design", an "outline" blanket or even a "comb" pattern. One name is as good as another, for it has definite characteristics of all.

Many colors are used in the whole piece. Attention should be directed to the arrangement of dark and light colors, as for example, dark at opposite sides of the outside row of triangles composing the center rhombus, and light at the other two. It may be noted, however, that the dark shade has been carried for about half the distance of one side of the low left hand side, and even into the base of the triangle where suddenly a lighter color was used. This kind of irregularity is common in all handmade objects which have much design.

The "fuzzy" blanket, which needs only the technical description I have given it, is not sufficiently prevalent to make it important in trade (Pl. VIII, *a*). It is, nevertheless, a definite style in Navajo blanket weaving.

The same may be said for the saddleblanket weaves. The styles used for these, exceptional for the Navajo, are determined by technical considerations which I have described in detail in the chapters on Pattern and Designing. From a commercial point of view they may be of small importance; from an artistic one they are not only interesting but some of them are excellent. Besides, they have considerable historical interest (see Chap. XVIII).

The edge is a part of the blanket which could be used as a decorative motive, and the most painstaking weavers consider it with care and prepare their twine accordingly. I have already referred to the possibilities it furnishes for unusual color combinations (p. 33). Only one blanket, however, of the many I have examined really exploits the edge. This is a blanket[1] of finely spun weft which has an edge of four heavy cords — black, white, red, and yellow — so manipulated as to form a noticeable and highly decorative border at the sides.

[1] Museum of the American Indian, Heye Foundation, 10/1510.

XVII Sandpainting Tapestries

The Navajo weaver, in early days and usually now when left to herself, will weave geometric designs. Once in a great while when she wishes to amuse herself she may try realism. One rug, for example, bore on its surface the evolution of transportation in the West. At its top was a pair of oxen, next two mules, then two automobiles and finally two aeroplanes. James reproduces a fearful and wonderful combination of designs of a railroad scene.[1] He relates the woman's story, her account of how she conceived it and why she wove it as she did. She seems to have had no motive except her own amusement.

When I showed this picture to my family, Marie remarked laughingly, "Some women weave designs like that that don't make any sense. . . .(mentioning a woman who receives very little for her blankets) always does. She is too lazy to think them out beforehand."

Marie's remark doubtless applies to some weavers but certainly not to the woman who wove this blanket if we are to credit James' story, for she was an expert. A fertile imagination may weary of conventional patterns and then a clever woman may just for fun, "play with her technique" and bring forth something of this sort. An indifferent worker would not apply herself consistently enough to make such a caricature.

Of the more serious realistic designs, birds and human beings sometimes occur, highly conventionalized forms with stiff, straight lines instead of contours. Generally the Navajo do not handle realistic subjects well (Pl. XV, *d, e*), and the Whites who try to influence them discourage such themes as much as possible. There is no rule to which there is no exception, and the Navajo with emphasis on extreme individualism often becomes the exception. A blanket depicting Shiprock in dull gray, black and white only is, in my opinion, worthy of

[1] Indian Blankets and their Makers, Fig. 146.

[*153*]

comparison with Old World tapestries. The picture is realistic; it has perspective and therefore good proportion; and, unlike that of Pl. XV, *e*, it is selective, using only Shiprock and the dike behind it as the theme. This blanket, the only realistic one I have ever seen which I consider successful, suggests that even the Navajo, given encouragement and practise, might succeed in developing tapestry as an art even as they have succeeded with the technique.

At the present time, when extreme pressure is being brought to bear on the modernizing of the Navajo, they are weaving a large number of the so-called "yeibichai (yaybichai)" blankets, the designs of which are hideous attempts at representation of the Navajo gods, ugly because false in every respect.

One of the important features of Navajo religion is the ritual of the masked gods. In it men appear garbed and painted as the Navajo believe the gods appear. These same deities may be represented in the beautiful soft-colored sandpaintings to which no medium of reproduction has yet done justice. The ritual and the paintings have captivated the imagination of many Whites, few of whom understand them. They have therefore encouraged the weaving of imitations (or substitutes) of the designs used for religious purposes.

There is no apparent reason why the designs should not be successful when executed in weaving. They are usually carried out in straight lines, although of course curves may easily be used in sand strewing. Generally, however, they are dismal failures. There are two reasons for the failure, one which I previously advanced as a cause for the main criticism of Navajo blankets, namely, color. More varied colors are used in sandpaintings than in other blankets and those the ones most difficult to achieve with such dyes as the Navajo have; blue, green, and pink give the most trouble. But there is a second major cause for the appearance of the "yei (yay)" blanket, and that is one which is almost universal. It is that the weaving technique is inappropriate and unsuitable to the carrying out of these designs.

The medicine man who superintends the laying of the superb sand-paintings on the floor of the hogan, and his assistants, work with such colors as they procure from natural sources, — the red-tan of the ordinary sand for background, white from chalk, black from soot or charcoal, red and yellow from iron oxides, blue and green from deposits containing copper salts. Besides these simple colors they use several which they mix, a gray-blue made with white and black; a pink made by combining red and white; and a dark brown made by mixing red and black. So far I know of no substitutes for these colors due to White influence. It is to be hoped there will be none. The colors cannot be combined in any way to make them ugly; they cannot be improved upon.

When the workers have their dry paints ready, they prepare a background of clean, earth-colored sand which they keep smoothing off with a batten as they work outward from the center of the picture. On this background they skilfully strew the designs by dropping the dry sand from between the two first fingers, controlling it by the thumb which rests lightly on the sand held between them. One of the numerous unusual features of the painting is the fact that there is no real erasing. If a mistake is made, it is obliterated by covering with natural-colored sand and dropping the correct color over it. It may be necessary for ceremonial reasons to use several layers of color. For example, the body of a deity's figure is made first. If he needs a garment, it is made by placing an additional layer of sand over the first. Some figures or parts of figures thus consist of many, sometimes as many as eight, colors. This fact accounts for the frequent sculptured or low-relief effect of some sandpaintings, as well as for the fact that they cannot be reproduced adequately and accurately by painting.

When Red Point paints, he uses the same technique. Needless to say, the finished product looks very different from the various stages in the painting process. With his paintbrush he outlined as hexagons the heads of the gods in one picture. When they were finished, they were all round and no one could have told they had ever been other-wise.

In weaving there can be, at least with such materials as the Navajo have to date, no satisfactory imitation in yarn of the colors which the sandpainters use. Likewise, there can be in the weaving technique no superposition of color unless it be by means of embroidery. Fur-thermore, accurate sandpaintings contain an unlimited amount of detail which is not entirely beyond the power of the weaver, but which few, indeed, can master. A third major fault is that the figures are grossly out of proportion, a matter which can be overcome by a good designer, but which rarely is.

Of the many "yay" blankets I have seen I have never seen one which had, in my opinion, the slightest claim to artistic value. I am aware that they are sold as extra-precious, at high prices. I also know that the Navajo do not like them. I know that they are rarely, if ever, conscientious reproductions of the figures of Navajo divinities. They look strange and esoteric; they must be valuable. That is the way the white buyer views them. Marie's comment upon the illustrations in James' book is, "Huh! I guess they never saw a sandpainting!"

If I seem to be unduly condemnatory, it is because I consider the "yay" blankets a perversion of the good technique of weaving and a prostitution of the noble art of sandpainting. There is another class of blankets, the "sandpainting" tapestries which must be discussed from a different angle. The source of design is the same, but instead of representing single or isolated repetitions of figures, they represent an actual sandpainting. Most of the blankets of this type one sees are subject to the same criticism as the "yay" blankets; they are gar-ishly colored, out of proportion, and badly managed technically. But there are rare exceptions; they may be compared with any tapestries.

The women who make them are expert, honest craftswomen. The men who design them are likewise conscientious. They draw or paint the composition on paper or cardboard; the women copy as faithfully as they can. The results are miraculous, if one may use that term for any of the Navajo fabrics. I have seen no evidence that a woman undertaking to make a sandpainting tapestry chooses a simple pattern or one having only straight lines, for example. She has faith in her ability to depict what she is given; she makes no bones about it, but works it out. If the painting happens to have much detail, as many do, it will be easier if the scale be large.

Consequently, the tapestry is set up on a huge loom. The fact of its size is a major problem, for it involves an endless amount of warp, skilful manipulation in setting it up and in tightening and changing its position ever after. All of these problems come up, however, in making any large blanket and if a woman can solve them for one sort she can do so for another.

The next greatest technical difficulty is also present for any large blanket, but it is greatly enhanced for the sandpaintings. That is the circumstance that a relatively small portion of the surface can be seen at once, so that it is difficult indeed to work out rhythm and symmetry and even harder to visualize the slight digressions from the usual rhythmic units.

Most women are satisfied to approximate the sandpaintings on a small surface and sales talk does the rest, but there are a few women who solve all these problems and the manner in which they do so is nothing short of astounding. Atlnaba is one. Her greatest pride is in weaving every detail. We once went to see another woman who was busy at a larger, more complicated one than Atlnaba was weaving at the time. It not only had many animal figures but each figure had no end of tiny details, some of which had ritualistic significance, others of which were merely decorative. Atlnaba's comment was, "She does not weave the little details in, she sews them on. It is not a good way, they will soon wear off."

She thus intimated that the woman was presenting an embroidered fabric for a woven one. I thought the sewing of the few small stitches quite justifiable. I thought, too, that Atlnaba might be slightly jealous, for much fuss was being made over this tapestry during the time it was being woven and after it was finished. I now think that motive must be considerably minimized for Atlnaba had woven tapestries quite as complicated and it is true there was not a stitch of any of hers that was not woven in.

High prices are paid for these tapestries. I feel that hardly any price is too high for them, because their value should be measured not only in effort which can scarcely be measured, so extensive is it, but also in emotion. The sandpainting is one of the many things in Navajo religion in which supernatural power inheres. Each one was given in the past by supernatural beings only to someone who had fasted, prayed and suffered so as to become worthy. That someone, a hero of the long myth which explains the entire ritual to which the sand-painting belongs, brought it back to his people. In some cases it was written originally on a cloud, in others, on a sacred buckskin, all kept in the possession of the gods. In every case it was brought to the Navajo written in the mind of the hero. He taught it to his people and for many years they have kept it in that form.

So important is the transitoriness of the sandpainting that it is used for only the shortest possible amount of time. It may take eighty-four hours — twelve men working seven hours — or longer, to make one. The first thing done with it when finished — it is sprinkled with cornmeal, and the Singer walks on it — ruins it. The entire per-formance done in its presence — for we, with the Navajo, may consider it sentient — is hurried, finished in as little time as possible, whereupon the sacred sand is gathered up and hastily disposed of. If treated in this way, its power will be for the good of all concerned, the singer, the person sung over, all his relatives, his house, his flocks, his corn, his land, all the audience, even of the Navajo as a people. But let a single act be out of place or irregular and the reverse effect may be expected.

If one can realize even fractionally how deeply religious belief, of which the sandpainting is only a small part, influences the behavior of the Navajo, he can begin to comprehend what it means to them to depict these things in a permanent medium like paper or tapestry. One can exert his mind even further and attempt to realize what it meant to the first person who broke the taboo of evanescence. As in the case of breaking any taboo, effects are watched for and relationships are made, misfortunes of one kind and another are ascribed to the "sin" of disobeying the gods. But, as is also the case when taboos become too burdensome, rationalizations are made.

A powerful singer has medicine in the form of prayers, rites and expiation which he can use to clear himself. This medicine has been given him to protect him from such mistakes as all humans are bound to make. The transition in the mind from an involuntary error to a voluntary one is not a great one and can be made easily by a good rationalizer. A medicine-man clears himself first with the supernaturals by use of the medicine. He must then prove to his fellows that his behavior is justified. The supernaturals are more easily satisfied! If he continues to live successfully, if he and his family have no "bad luck" for a long time, he may convince his people to a degree. However, there will be some who, identifying obstinacy with orthodoxy, will consider success following tampering with the supernatural as witchcraft. If this happens, a singer will have to prove his intimacy and favoritism with the gods even further. Only fate can decide the issue. Practically it remains eternally undecided. The accusation of witchcraft is a perfect resolvent of jealousy.

Not only can the singer exonerate himself before his supernatural beings but he may use his power on others. Consequently, if a woman who has woven a sandpainting becomes ill or incapacitated in any way, she may be cured by having a "sing". The fact that she needs one is, of course, the proof of the layman's orthodoxy. One of the most famous sandpainting weavers was dying of cancer. She had had many sings to cure her offense in weaving the sandpaintings. After each one she became a little better. The cure continued as long as the disease allowed her to survive. Its final futility has proved the Navajo religion right.

Another sort of rationalization is made to legalize the permanency of the paintings. This one is often made by such sandpainters as demonstrate their skill in department stores, fairs, hotels, and museums. The curse is upon the misuse of accurate sandpaintings. It is easy enough to be well paid for making the paintings and, as long as they are not absolutely as the gods described, they may not be dangerous. Thus, a god may be depicted with three feathers on his headdress instead of four; the colors of a bow may be interchanged, for example, a red one which should have blue markings may be decorated in black. The digressions made are usually, from our point of view, insignificant enough; in my opinion they are thoroughly justified.

A weaver of sandpainting tapestry may defend herself by having a complete nine-day "sing" of the chant she is weaving. When least elaborate it will cost from $200 to $400. This is an additional reason for the high price of a genuine sandpainting. Hastin Gani's Wife, before she began to weave paintings from the Shooting Chant, had that chant "sung over her". Since that time she is able to weave any one of the many symbolic compositions with a reasonable amount of safety. She offends, however, in another direction, according to the old orthodoxy.

The Navajo used to believe it was "not good" to overdo. That meant moderation in all things. A medicine-man must not sing his chant too often without renewing his power; no one should use his name often lest he wear out its ability to help him out of trouble; a woman should not complete a blanket, no matter how small in one day. She should leave a bit to finish on the morrow. I found no sentiment against overdoing at Ganado. The achievement of Hastin Gani's Wife in finishing her huge blanket in a month was acclaimed with complacent pride by all concerned.

I have been speaking exclusively of women who weave the elaborate designs, either of the ordinary large rugs or of the sandpainting tapestries. In contrast to the Hopi and Zuñi it is the women among the Navajo who do most of the weaving. There are among them, however, a few male weavers whose work is of the best. If a Navajo man weaves, he is put in the class of "man-woman", a category sanctioned as including such men as want to carry on woman's activities, or such men as one of my informants said who "do not likes women". Left-Handed-Singer of Newcomb is the only one of this sort whom I know personally. He is well known by Whites and Navajo and is greatly respected. He is an extraordinarily interesting character; he has a superior type of intelligence combined with extreme gentleness, and at the same time he is remarkably independent. He weaves only sandpainting tapestries. Being an accomplished singer, he weaves the designs "out of his own head". Men who weave do not by any means restrict their weaving to the religious designs, although they are likely to be learned in medicine.

In the face of the emotional and social pressure exerted it is easy to understand why the number of Navajo who weave the sandpainting rugs, and who weave them constantly better, more elaborately and more accurately, is increasing. One reason may well be the challenge of competition. "If that woman, a friend of mine and a good weaver though no better than I, can make such a tapestry, why should I not do the same?" Then, too, the dollar, dangling at the end of a string pulled ever shorter and shorter, has the same effect on the Navajo as upon ourselves. It supersedes all other values, be they social, moral or spiritual.

XVIII Origin and Age

In discussing the style of the Navajo blanket I had intended to keep history and style distinct. When one views superficially the rank and file of old and modern blankets it seems as if such a distinction could be made. The differences are, however, more apparent than real. They are really complex developments of old ideas upon which new ones have been grafted.

In any discussion or description of a process as involved as that of weaving, it is to be expected that different observers will disagree upon various questions. This is especially true when the questions deal with a people as numerous, versatile, and individualistic as the Navajo. They are spread over such a wide area and each family lives in such comparative independence that local differences are to be expected. Besides, each locality has been exposed for many decades to diverse influences. Roughly speaking, three large regions may be distinguished as set off one from another, the area east of the Chuskai-Lukachukai-Tunicha range of mountains; that west of the mountain chain, extending to Black Mountain; and a third, west of Black Mountain, extending to the Hopi country.

Of these regions the central comes nearest to pursuing ancient Navajo ways of living, beliefs and standards. The district is of course only roughly defined but includes the northernmost part of the Reservation and even the western slopes of the Black Mountain district and the adjoining plain. Closely related to this division is the section from Keam's Cañon westward to the Reservation limits. Superimposed on the old Navajo ways in this region and so thoroughly amalgamated with them as to be hardly distinguishable at times, are Hopi ideas carried out always in a Navajo way. In the district east of the Chuskai-Lukachukai range, a large part of which is included by the Shiprock and Chaco regions, there is more sophistication than elsewhere. Here and in the entire territory of the Santa Fe railroad inhabited by the Navajo, white influence has taken strong hold and Americanization is making rapid strides. As a result the Navajo are in that difficult transitional stage of instability commonly found when "civilizing" has "advanced" to a particular point. Change is taking place so rapidly that individuals question both the old and the new and are undecided as to which course to pursue. Some cling to the old, some try to take up the new, and many have few beliefs or modes of action on which they can rely.

It is easy to understand then, why one observer gets a particular answer to a question and why another gets one which is anywhere from slightly different to utterly incompatible. It is also probable that the amount of time put upon the question may account for the differences in the answers.

I have repeatedly observed that reality among natives is frequently, as among ourselves, quite the contrary to what they state as being generally true. Marie, for example, told me that Navajo women *never* sleep in the daytime, but in my four summers of residence with her family I have sometimes found her and her female housemates asleep in the daytime. True, it may have been the day after an all-night vigil, or the woman in question may have been ill, nevertheless she was sleeping in the daytime. Again, Marie says no good weaver pounds down her weft with the batten. She, her mother, and sisters never do, yet I have seen many excellent weavers do so. Those who do are more numerous than those who do not, so many are they, in fact, that I suspect the prejudice against the practise is a family peculiarity.

In my opinion, there is no absoluteness of truth about Navajo affairs. Often one fact is as true as another, even though it be different. If we could accept this circumstance, we should come much nearer to a Navajo attitude, "Yes, So-and-So always does it that way, but I always do it this way. His way is all right for him, my way is best for me."

[163]

The question of the origin and age of the Navajo blanket is one upon which there are many opinions. As I have said, I am more interested in the modern weaver than in her blanket; more in what she thinks as she works, than in speculations about her remote ancestors. It would be unnatural, however, to dismiss from consideration the ever-stimulating question concerning all cultural problems, "How did it all come about?"

[Since I wrote this chapter in the winter of 1933 Charles Amsden's book, Navaho Weaving, has appeared. Since this book deals primarily with history and with the relationship between development and technique I am abbreviating my remarks. I feel justified, however, in including this small part of the discussion since it seems to me of sufficient methodological interest that two investigators, each fastening upon himself the controls furnished by evidence as objective as he can make it, should come to approximately the same conclusions.]

Before we can determine the origin of the art of weaving, we must consider its age. In my opinion, there is no incontrovertible and irrefutable evidence of any Navajo woolen blanket which is more than one hundred years old [Cp. Wyman & Amsden, A Patchwork Cloak, The Masterkey, Volume VIII (September 1934): 133]. I am aware that stories which purport to be on good authority are extant setting the age of certain blankets at two hundred and fifty or three hundred years. I know the stories and in each one there is a period which is highly mythological. With the utmost generosity I must set that period as ending not earlier than one hundred or at best one hundred and fifty years ago.

If we admit that the oldest blankets we know of are no more than one hundred years old, we must emphatically note, too, that the blankets of that earliest period represent technically and artistically the best, which means that at that time the art of weaving was fully developed. The weaving industry has advanced rapidly indeed among the Navajo since we have actual history on it. It is not reasonable to suppose that it progressed with equal rapidity from the time of its origin. By allowing for the probable slowness of development in its initial stages we may conservatively set the approximate time of its origin at about 1780 which is the time when we have the first report of Navajo settlement west as far as the Chuskai Mountains.[1]

The exact period when the Navajo first procured sheep is debatable, but since their entire early history is a tale of raiding both neighboring Indian tribes and Whites, it is more than likely that they had or knew sheep and the use of wool many years before the old blankets were made.[2] The question of the probable sources of Navajo weaving knowledge arises simultaneously with that of age.

Some assert that the Navajo are descendants of the prehistoric people of the Southwest and that, therefore, they learned the art of weaving from them. All that is needed to complete this argument is that they transferred the art of treating cotton to wool and the explanation is complete. But we must consider that all the direct evidence points to the fact that the Navajo are newcomers to the Southwest; five hundred years is doutbless too liberal an allowance for their sojourn in the region. Half a millenium is an insufficient time allowance for close relationships with the early prehistoric peoples, for the largest of their populations, those in the Chaco and Mesa Verde regions, for example, were extinct as early as the thirteenth century. In the case of others there is the possibility of continuity (not definitely proved for any group) with the present day Pueblo Indians.

There are also persons who dismiss the question of origin of the Navajo blanket briefly as an art learned from the Spanish. The fact that wool, the material upon which it depends, is a gift of the Whites to the Navajo is one which favors the supposition at least superficially. Add to it the fact that most of the oldest blankets we

[1] Report of Commander General of the Interior Provinces of New Spain, 1786.
[2] See Bartlett, K. Museum Notes, Museum of Northern Arizona, Volume 5 (December 1932): 30.

know are woven from materials furnished by Whites, the baizes, Saxony and Germantown yarns, and the argument is strengthened. To my mind there is, however, a serious objection to adopting this as a final conclusion. This is the technique. The entire process of rug manufacture, from spinning to the finished product, is American in style.

The most widely used European loom is horizontal and is distinguished from the vertical one by the use of rigid healds of reed, wood, or metal. The principle most commonly in use is that of throwing the woof across the entire width of the shed. These essential principles are not unknown in the Southwest. The Zuñi, for example, use a reed harness; even the Navajo throw the woof across the web for the saddle-blanket weaves.

On the other hand, the upright loom was known in Greece as early as 200 B. C. and there is no reason to believe that there was any discontinuity in its use sufficient to cause a lapse in the knowledge of how to use it. Its appearance is sporadic in Europe, but it was known and used in the regions from which the Spaniards, the earliest settlers of the Southwest, came. However, the European loom even at its simplest, involves the use of more machinery — shuttles, bobbins, rolls instead of loops to make sheds — than does that of the Southwest. The tapestry art of southern Europe also involves sewing to a great extent, although the Norwegians manipulate warp and weft in a special fashion in joining their design elements.

It seems to me that these differences are so fundamental that they would be present, even if only vestigially, among the Navajo if they had learned weaving from the Europeans. I believe that Navajo weaving is a native American art. The art of weaving on an upright loom has been continuous in the Southwest for centuries. At first there was a wide variety of basket and mat weaves which did not involve a loom. We do not know much about the earliest looms except the fact that they existed. Several prehistoric finds point to arrangements for fastening a loom firmly to the floor of a room [Cp. Amsden, p. 25]. A number of woven fabrics taken from prehistoric sites show a high development of loom weaving. Most of them are made of animal or human hair, of string made from vegetable fibers, or of cotton.

Many of the contemporary Pueblo tribes weave on the same kind of loom as the Navajo and use cotton, as well as woolen yarns. In pre-Spanish days some of the Pueblos raised their own cotton; there is no proof that the Navajo ever did. Although our earliest accounts show the Navajo in contact with the eastern Pueblos (Jemez) and the Spanish at the same time, it is reasonable to suppose that they had more intimate knowledge of the customs and arts of their Indian, than of their White neighbors. Few of the eastern Pueblos practised the art of weaving at this early date. It is probable there were Navajo contacts, either predatory or even more permanent, as far west as the Hopi country which were never reported. The rough and unfriendly geographical conditions, the brevity of contact between those making the reports and the Indians, as well as their strictly military interest, are reasons against their securing such information.

In addition to the material furnished by prehistory, there are indications that weaving may have been nearly continuous in distribution from the Tlingit of the extreme Northwest to the Southwest with the Salish as a point of transition. The chain of proof is not continuous, but each new bit of knowledge corroborates the theory. In 1926 the Museum of the American Indian, Heye Foundation[1] published a description of a Salish blanket which suggests comparison with the Navajo. Viewed superficially, the blanket could be Navajo. The composition is not very common to Navajo, but the elements are all typical. It is executed in a twining technique which does not belong to loom weaving. The end bindings of the Navajo rug are twined and the edges are given the same effect although it, being vertical instead of horizontal, is secured in a different way. The edges are a point at

[1] Leaflet Number 5.

which differentiation between Navajo and Pueblo weaving is made. Fine textiles[1], however, from the White House Ruin of Cañon de Chelley, apparently not made of animal fiber, have the binding and edge exactly like the Navajo, showing that it must be much older in the Southwest than Navajo weaving.

Another feature of the Salish blanket must be noted, i. e., some of the design elements are worked in a diagonal direction instead of straight across the warp. This manipulation may correspond to that which the Navajo used to employ in making the "scalloped" blanket (see p. 118) in which a diagonal was woven instead of a horizontal design. It is, for the Navajo, an old technique, one which apparently never established a firm position for itself, for it had a weakness which is now considered a mistake, if not a joke.

A number of similarities having to do with culture in general, rather than with weaving, can be shown to exist between the Northwest and the Navajo, and they are not astounding considering the close linguistic affiliations between the Navajo and the Northern Athapascans. There are, for instance, ceremonial details whose southern ascertainable limit in the North is among the Thompson band which assimilated an Athapascan group. It is beyond the scope of this discussion to include these details, some of which are astonishingly similar, but I should like to point out a combination of details which seems to me significant. The yellow yarn of the Chilkat blanket was dyed by boiling a lichen in the *fresh urine of children.* Compare this with the old Navajo belief that indigo was successful only if used in the urine of very young (and consequently pure) children.

It is a Northwestern belief that certain matters, dependent upon supernatural volition, the attainment of a guardian spirit, for instance, have no validity if experienced by a person no longer chaste. The distribution of this belief is not continuous from the Northwest into

[1] American Museum of Natural History.

the Southwest, and it may well be that the Navajo brought it with them, although they have changed its interpretation greatly.

For these reasons I had concluded that weaving was an art known over a large, and perhaps continuous, area from the Tlingit in the far north to the Southwest. The prehistoric peoples of the South contributed the principle of the harness to separate the warp. This invention, one of the most important in weaving, caused development in an entirely different direction. This may well have been due to influence from still farther South—Mexico, for example. Consequently, I had intended to say at a symposium held at Andover in December 1935, that, in my opinion, the Navajo were familiar with weaving, though perhaps not weavers, when they came to the Southwest. Not that they introduced it into that region, but rather that when they came, they were so familiar with the notion, that they took to it with the alacrity demonstrated by the earliest efforts known to us.

The reader can imagine, therefore, my surprise and pleasure at hearing the remarks of Dr. A. V. Kidder in his short paper, "The Navajo in the Light of Archaeology", which in summary were as follows: "The pottery of the Navajo is like no pottery of the Southwest, but shows a resemblance to archaeological pottery finds of western Nebraska.[1] For this reason, I conclude that the Navajo brought with them the knowledge and technique of pottery-making, rather than that they learned it from the other people of the Southwest."

In reconstructions of this sort, hints serve for speculation and there are great discrepancies in time and space. I believe the presence of the weaving techniques now used by the Navajo in prehistoric times, and the fact that the Pueblo Indians use every type known to the Navajo, shows that the newcomers were imitators and adapters, but did not hesitate to modify the ideas which they picked up.

---

[1] The Navajo have many traits in common with the western Plains.

One technical fact, which the ancient people of the Southwest (Basketmakers?) had in common with the North and in contrast to the Navajo, is that they used many-ply[1] yarn, whereas the Navajo have employed it only when it was furnished by Whites. They know how to make it, but use it only for bindings, never for weft and not even for warp. This fact points, I believe, to the Navajo relearning of weaving upon entering the Southwest and securing wool, a new material.

The relationship of the Navajo blanket to those of other peoples of the Southwest is manifest. Some Navajo blankets, particularly old ones, are so similar to Hopi blankets that some experts, whose knowledge comes from painstaking study and frequent handling of many blankets, like Mrs. Mary R. Colton, for example, confess that they cannot tell accurately if they are Hopi or Navajo. Such correspondence is not to be wondered at when the close contiguity and long period of reciprocal influence are taken into consideration. It is almost certain that Pueblo weaving will be traced to Mexico for the source of its origin, but I must leave that problem to those primarily interested in the weaving of the Pueblo Indians.

In my opinion the "fancy" or "saddleblanket" weaves furnish the best explanation of historical relationships which we may expect from a study of technique. My remarks on this subject are based primarily on facts secured in learning to weave the various patterns. [At certain points in this part of my discussion I am forced to disagree with Mr. Amsden.]

The earliest account of Navajo weaving which even hints at an understanding of its complexity is that of Matthews[2] published in 1885. In this short treatise he somewhat categorically mentions diagonal cloth and cloth of diaper weave. The few details he gives are not sufficient to teach the weaves, but the record shows that they

[1] According to Orchard (A Rare Salish Blanket, 7), the Salish used eight-ply yarn for warp and three-ply and five-ply for weft. It is likely that there was considerable variation in different fabrics and even in the same piece.
[2] Report Bureau of American Ethnology 3 (1881-82): 371—391.

were known and liked more than fifty years ago, doubtless for a much longer time. There is no apparent difference between those made in Matthews' time and those of today.

Of greater age is the patchwork cloak described by Wyman and Amsden[1] found as a Navajo shroud and estimated to be at least a hundred years old. This cloak shows remnants of diaper cloth (diamond) and a kind of twilling (variation of braided), of ordinary weaving, of "beading", and one of a weave which from the description "a checkerboard pattern in which half the blocks are in plain black, the remainder of short stripes in green and blue, each block being slightly under two inches square" suggests to me the setup for the double-faced blanket of Pl. XI, *a*. Even though Amsden considers the remnant in diaper pattern of Pueblo origin, the burial shows that the Navajo knew it and used it at a time much earlier than we have previously been able to prove.

The stress laid on the scarcity of the saddleblankets is more theoretical than real. Many women know how to make them, few know them all, but since these types do not come into trade as such, little is said about them. Most traders do not know the difference between these and other weaves and the few that arrive at a blanket-room are often lost among the piles of the ordinary ones. All this has nothing to do with Navajo knowledge and distinction of them.

The diagonal weaves, "braided" and "diamond", are mere modifications of Hopi weaves. The difference between Navajo and Hopi is stylistic rather than technical. The conservative Hopi use few quiet colors and display practically no versatility in their weaving. Their conservatism has led to the development of fine materials and extreme finish of fabric. They use the diagonal technique widely but since it is usually in self-color, it is not related to Navajo "braided" in the layman's mind. In the same way the Hopi "diamond" becomes diaper cloth whereas the Navajo is an interesting and unique three-color

[1] The Masterkey, Volume VIII (1934): 133—137.

pattern. Differences of this sort are cultural and psychological. The Pueblo, being conservative in every way, is interested in finish while preserving design and effect; the Navajo, daring in weaving as in all other phases of his culture, makes new departures. Consequently, although he is essentially an imitator, he develops something which becomes peculiarly his own, sometimes so disguised as to make its source confusing.

As I eagerly await the account of Mrs. Mary R. Colton on Hopi weaving, I regret greatly that I can make no detailed comparison of Hopi and Navajo weaving. There is reason to believe that the principles of Hopi and Zuñi weaving are nearly identical and I shall summarize the similarity between Navajo procedure and Zuñi as far as possible.[1] The Zuñi use three methods of spinning. One is the same as the Navajo use for spinning weft, the other a modification of the method of rolling on the thigh which the Navajo have adopted for twisting double-ply yarn. I have never seen the Navajo tighten the twist by the third method in which the foot is used by Zuñi and Hopi.

There is no essential difference in the looms of Hopi, Zuñi and Navajo. All have the broad stationary loom and the belt loom. I detect only one difference in the manipulation of the loom for the twilled self-color as described by Spier. It is the introduction of a rod to form a "temporary shed after the free (heald) rod has been raised." I do not understand this but it may take the place of the additional temporary rod in making the shed of the belt (Chapter XV, p. 136).

Spier notes that the Zuñi weave six inches from bottom, up, then reverse the loom and weave again from bottom up, a matter which necessitates reversing the four healds making the twill, if the diagonals are to be continuous for the entire length of the blanket instead of forming a chevron at the center. Even this sort of manipulation is used by the Navajo but for a different purpose. Alice Curley, when weaving

---

[1] The details of Zuñi weaving are taken from the short but excellent article *Zuñi Weaving Technique* by Leslie Spier, American Anthropologist 26 (1924): 64—85.

a chief blanket, turned it after a time so she could fit her design more exactly into the space (Pl. VI, *c*).

The double-faced blanket which is the most astonishing result of the warp manipulation had Matthews[1] more than puzzled in 1890. He believed, because he had never seen any in his former sojourn among the Navajo from 1880 to 1884, that the type did not exist at that time, but had been invented between 1884 and 1890 when he returned and saw it. I do not believe the fact that he did not see it and that Mr. Keam who lived with the Navajo since about 1870 did not see it, absolute proof that it did not exist. There are traders on the Reservation today who do not realize its existence. Matthews and Keam were both observant and discerning men, but the most dangerous remark to make about the Navajo is that they "do not have it" or they "do not do it". They have and do many things that they do not see fit to report. They are not secretive like their Pueblo neighbors but either they do not think the Whites would be interested, or they consider an affair too obvious or casual for remark. Consequently all negative statements must be subjected to constant reconsideration.

The double-faced blanket is not a difficult achievement once the setup of the warp is understood. It is not easy to explain exactly how a person may have happened upon it, but once she started experimenting it is not as difficult to arrive at as some of the more common weaves. Mr. J. L. Hubbell had a huge rug (Pl. XII, *b*) of this sort which may have been made as early as 1886.[2] Its very size (twelve feet four inches by eighteen feet two inches) points to an argument for either side of the case. A rug as large as this is extraordinarily unwieldy to manage no matter what technique is used. The fact that it was reasonably well done shows its maker was a virtuoso. If a woman could handle warp of such size at all, she would have no more difficulty

[1] American Anthropologist 2 (1900): 638—642.
[2] Now in the possession of Mr. B. I. Staples of Coolidge, New Mexico, to whose kindness I owe the accompanying photograph.

making the two-faced cloth than she would with the ordinary weave. It is reasonable to suppose she had full confidence in herself and that it was not the first she had ever done, or she would never have undertaken a matter so pretentious.

On the other hand, it may be argued that this weave had become a new style at the time Matthews mentions, 1884-1890. If that were true, it is not unthinkable that interest, centered on the new style, encouraged a woman to "play with the technique" and that control would thus express itself in great size even as it does today among the weavers at Ganado.

The date of the first appearance of the weave is still doubtful. It was never a popular one, but was always considered unique. At the present time it is amusing to all the weavers I know. Although double-faced blankets are rare it is not at all difficult to find women who know how to weave them. Matthews writes that he cannot analyze the principle from the loom he illustrates in the short article cited. The first two looms I saw on which blankets of this sort were strung were purposely falsified by the workers, "so another woman could not learn from them", explained the woman who helped me with it. I can hardly believe that the same kind of duplicity was practised on Matthews forty years ago. On the other hand, I do not see how he could have missed the point had his loom been properly strung, for, if we are to judge by his treatise on the diagonal weaves,[1] he understood them and this is no more difficult.

Speculations have been advanced as to the origin of this weave. Matthews considers it unqualifiedly Navajo since he knows of no other place on the earth's surface where it occurs. The only contribution James makes is that sometimes as many as eight healds are used, but he does not illustrate any blanket made with that many, nor does he say he ever saw one. [Amsden is of the opinion "that the machine-made figured Pendleton blanket, so common in modern Navajo dress

[1] Report of the Bureau of American Ethnology 3.

[*174*]

is a counterpart of the two-faced type and I strongly suspect it of being the father of the Navajo product" (p. 62). This seemed to me highly improbable since machine-woven fabrics are merely reversed in color, few of them, the so-called golf cloths (including steamer rugs) have two entirely different designs on the two sides. The Pendleton blankets I have seen have only reverse patterns, as is to be expected of machine-made materials. If, for example, the ground is black and the design orange on one side, the opposite side will have the same pattern in black on an orange ground. This is a very different thing from, for example, a triangular design on the face and a striped composition, or even a plain one, on the back.

A letter from Mr. Melvin D. Fell of the Pendleton Woolen Mills removes my doubt as to the experience of the Navajo with double-faced Pendleton blankets. "To the best of our knowledge we have never made a double-faced blanket in a commercial way. Years ago there may have been some experiment along that line but I am sure there was no quantity made."]

I believe that the Navajo secured the idea from the Hopi and, as is the case with so many other details of their culture, revamped it according to their own lights.

In making his "embroidery weave" the Hopi weaver throws his shed, then casts a strand of self-color weft across the entire width of his loom. He then reaches to the back of the loom where his loose and vari-colored threads hang, picks them up one by one and weaves them about the proper strands of his warp. The hint the original Navajo needed was the throwing of the self-color which takes its place a little above but also behind the row already in the web. At that the Navajo manipulation is a simpler one than that of the Hopi, which at the same time achieves an entirely different result. For the Navajo throws her weft through the shed as she would in any other style of weaving; the Hopi wraps his additional strand *around* the warps, thus giving it a raised embroidered appearance. The Hopi sash has only one face; the back of it, also a modified reverse pattern, is unfinished showing that its maker has no interest in it. In spite of all these differences which are of effect only, the sash-weaver probably furnished the initial inspiration which yielded, after treatment by the versatile and adaptive mind and skilful fingers of the Navajo craftswoman, the double-faced cloth.

Several facts account for the Spanish or European elements in the oldest blankets. The first contacts of the Navajo with Indians and Whites alike were hostile. All the early accounts are narratives of raids, and in the tales domesticated animals are mentioned. The step from raiding for food to subsequently using the fleece of the animals taken is not a long one, especially when made in the region where an example was constantly before the eyes. The fact that we know of no cotton blankets made by the Navajo strengthens the opinion that acquaintance with sheep and knowledge of weaving were coincident or nearly so [Cp. Amsden, p. 31, 32].

But the Navajo were not only aggressors in this medley of influences. Though they made raids, when they came into territory more thickly populated by Whites they were conquered, individually, if not as a tribe. There seems to be no doubt that many Navajo — some estimate three thousand — were slaves to Spanish and Mexican families of the Southwest. They were, furthermore, valued slaves. Women served more numerously in this capacity than men. The stories told of the weaving of the old blankets refer to the period when this subservience was at its peak (about 1830-1860). Families, which valued their slaves at $ 300 to $ 400, were those which wore good clothes. They were the ones who furnished the elegant materials to their weavers. They probably knew the art of weaving, may even have practised it themselves. It is more likely that they were patrons, rather than executors, of the art.

During the years I have been studying Navajo weaving I have had need to revise my opinion of its origin many times. At no time, however, have I doubted that it is an American, and not a European, art. The evidence, in my opinion, points to the Navajo being exposed to weaving, perhaps with a loom but not one with healds, in their wanderings from the north to the south. I do not consider the case of Navajo descent from the prehistoric peoples of the Southwest strong. There is too great a discrepancy in time between their cultural development and that of the Navajo. Consequently, I think that the Navajo, susceptible to the idea of weaving, but perhaps not having contributed anything toward it, upon entering the Southwest, took it over from their Pueblo neighbors and developed it in their own way.

The Pueblos were doubtless inhospitable to the Navajo, but helpless enough before them. As the Navajo pushed onward in the Southwest they encountered Whites, mounted and armed, with horses and weapons difficult to oppose. Many of the raiders were taken as prisoners and their women put to work. The ability to weave was an important item in determining their value. They were given good materials and allowed to weave. The results are the fine old blankets we know today, and the whole development of Navajo weaving, a distinct contribution to art and to the culture of the Southwest.

XIX Symbolism

A question most frequently asked of those interested in the Navajo blanket is, "But what does it *mean*?" The question is asked also of designs on silver and other objects native to the Southwest. There is something in our own way of thought, perhaps indefinable, which demands symbolism. We have little of our own, what we have is frequently puerile; nevertheless, we insist on it in our Indian products. Some insistent Whites who do not find it among our Indians resort to that ever-useful argument, which no scientist can answer, "But it must previously have been there and now it is lost."

Before discussing the matter of symbolism for the Navajo I shall give my definition of it. A symbol is, in my opinion, a design unit, or even an entire composition, which has a definite emotional content or meaning, immediately and spontaneously recognized by a group of people. This, I am perfectly aware, leaves out of consideration "individual" symbolism. That is something we must leave to our poets and psychoanalysts for it can be nothing more than a guessing game for the audience. That individual Navajo women may "read meaning" into their own designs is possible; it is even to be expected. I am concerned with the more general reactions of the group.

The answer to the question, "What does it mean?" is simply, "Nothing". The patterns the weavers use sometimes have names, although naming even is slightly developed among Navajo as compared with other craftswomen, for example, the basket weavers of northern California. Even such names as exist are singularly unpoetic. In Fig. 32 *a* is "like a card"; *b*, *c* "like a slingshot", or "big star" for rhombus or square standing on a point. A Roman cross, *d*, is "sticks crossing each other", *e*, a St. Andrew's, "a star". The hourglass unit, *f*, is simply a "queue", the unit made up of vertical lines broken by horizontal ones, *j*, is termed "row of empty spaces set

Fig. 32

off in zigzag order". This term is interesting because it defines the space rather than the lines which bound it.

I might continue the list of elements, but with few exceptions, which I shall note, they are named in the same unromantically descriptive fashion. The same is true of combinations of the initial units, Fig. 32, *g*, "a square within a square"; *h*, "diamond within diamond", "large empty spaces (terrace edged diamond) follow each other", *i*, "squares (or triangles) follow and touch each other".

There are several units which seem to be generally symbolic for the Southwest, although as they are used by the Navajo in blankets and on silver they have little emotional content. They are the "cloud terrace", the zigzag, the name of which shows a relationship to the word for "lightning"—whether the one is from the other or the other from the one, it is impossible to say. The swastika is a ubiquitous element of design which in Navajo religion has symbolic importance. But in weaving and silverwork it is called merely "that which revolves". Similarly, paired rows of chevrons are called "tracks", but their components in a single row, *l*, are merely "pointed ones following one another", and if a row should be made where one set is turned in one direction, the other in the opposite, and they dovetail (Fig. 32, *k*), they are called "sticking in the opposite direction". The distinction between pure description and poetic fancy is not carefully drawn, but in this field the mundane triumphs over the imaginative.

A word should be said about the more realistic designs. The bow and arrow are often used, and recently on silver, a bird called "thunderbird" by purchasing Whites. These designs, as well as some of the more simple geometric ones, have true symbolism in Navajo religion. When they are used as parts of sandpaintings or on rattles or other paraphernalia of the medicine-man, they have a deep, an awe-inspiring, emotional appeal. The bow is thought of as the magic bow of the mythic hero and war god, "Slayer-of-the-Alien-Gods", the arrow may be that of his powerful brother, "Child-of-the-Water".

Thunder, in the form of a figure slightly resembling a bird is used, too, but it has faint resemblance to the "thunderbird" of trade pieces.

In the sandpaintings a chevron is "deer track" and very important. A kind of swastika may be "whirling logs" which are of major significance in more than one myth. There are a number of lightning symbols "straight", "sheet", or "zigzag". Strangely, though the Navajo *call* the terraced triangle "cloud image" (Fig. 33, *b*) they *symbolize* clouds by a succession of triangles one superimposed upon the

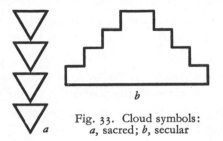

Fig. 33. Cloud symbols:
a, sacred; *b*, secular

other (Fig. 33, *a*). The Roman cross is of great ceremonial importance. Cornmeal, pollen, and other sacred substances are strewn in the form of a Roman cross and often the same figure forms the fundamental basis upon which the sandpainting is laid out. It means direction, east to west for one part of the cross, south to north for the other.

There may be also a subsidiary St. Andrew's cross, the parts of which mark off the intermediate directions, southeast, southwest, northwest, and northeast.

These illustrations selected from a vast number of possible ones explain, I think, the lack of imagination with regard to designs used on things the Navajo sell (let it be remembered I do not deny the possibility of individual symbolism). They have a well-worked-out symbolism with functions generally understood in their religious life. What I said previously about sandpaintings applies here as well. These symbols represent to the people who believe in them, supernatural power. That power may be mistreated; if it is used too much, it "wears out". Who, understanding this attitude, would expect its owners to give it away? For that is what selling a blanket or a piece. of silver with "sacred patterns" means. In this attitude the conflict arising from weaving sandpaintings germinates and will continue to flourish until belief is entirely undermined.

It seems to me that this matter of symbolism serves as an indirect check to my theory of origin. We know that silverwork is a late art with the Navajo; all the materials must be furnished from the outside. I have shown that weaving is also relatively late, and that early in its development it was greatly influenced by other phases of culture. It seems reasonable, therefore, to conclude that the new arts which, when all is said and done, were taken over mainly for economic reasons, never became thoroughly worked into the spiritual life of the tribe. The fact of their lateness is not conclusive. The horse was also a late acquisition but it is so completely woven into Navajo mythology that a layman would not know that there ever was a time they did not have it. The explanation must be found deeper in Navajo thought. The horse became something truly theirs. After a Navajo acquired one, it was his. He had droves of horses but he traded them among his own people. They did not go to aliens if he could help it. With weaving and silversmithing it was different. True blankets were used by the natives themselves, but there was always a lively trade, and it is likely the first ones were made for Whites. The Navajo themselves wore silver ornaments, but they always represented a foreign means of exchange.

For these, and possibly other reasons, the designs on trade objects never became packed with the emotional content typical of their most important activity, religion. The condition is comparable to one we might ourselves experience. A person who has no religion, who may even be a "queen of scoffers" may wear a crucifix. Its workmanship perhaps, or its material may have appealed to her. Or, perchance, it is a souvenir of a memorable party in Italy which gives her constant pleasure. The crucifix is a symbol familiar to, if not understood by, even the ungodly. The value of it as an art object may depend upon the individual who wears it, may have nothing at all to do with its general or original symbolism. In the same way I think the Navajo have kept the symbolic designs of their religion apart, in a separate compartment of their minds, from their ordinary blanket and silver-work patterns. The *form* occasionally overlaps; the emotions are kept distinct.

XX Opinions

I have touched only lightly upon the two questions in which many writers and collectors are primarily interested. I have given cause for my sketchy treatment of origin and age and at the same time I have stated my opinion in the matter.

I am not by any means immune to the symbolism controversy. However, I have long since been convinced, by extended studies in other fields of primitive art, that our idea of symbolism is neither necessary nor absolute, that the symbol most closely packed with emotional value may be an old piece of string or some other object we should hardly know exists. If we do learn of it, we may choose to ignore it because it does not appeal to our aesthetic ideals. I have learned, too, that the same native to whom the treatment of that greasy bit of string may mean emotional life or death, may at the same time be the carver of a bit of wood which causes the most exacting connoisseur to gasp with pleased amazement. The native may have no feeling at all about it, except the satisfaction of having made it. For this reason I must depend on the reactions of the natives themselves rather than upon a romancer with a preconceived bias. The reaction of the Navajo to "sold" designs, according to my experience, is as I have stated.

There are several other matters about which previous authors disagree, and a few which depend on the rationale of the weavers themselves. A misconception which prevails in all the older accounts and even in the minds of those intimately acquainted with the Navajo is the question of wool cleansing. I have referred to it in the chapters on Wool (Chapter II) and Color (Chapter IV). It is commonly believed that the wool is washed immediately after shearing or at least before any other process is undertaken. This is the case only when the wool is unusually greasy or dirty, so disagreeable as to make handling uncomfortable. A woman uses wool like this only rarely, avoids it when possible (which means usually); consequently, it is the exception rather than the rule. The fact is that the wool is most often cleaned by the cards and fingers of the carder and spinner, and not washed at all until it is in the form of yarn. Furthermore, if it happens to be destined for color or for warp, it is *not washed at all*. Dyeing to the Navajo mind takes the place of washing.

There are several reasons for non-extensive washing. In the first place, the wool itself is not greasy or offensively dirty. In the second, the Navajo is by training, habit and necessity a water saver. She considers water water. Is dye not mostly water? Why then should one waste an additional amount of it washing the wool when it will have a bath in the dye anyhow? Finally, she is ignorant of the chemical properties of the dyes she uses. She knows greasy wool will not dye as well as that which is not. But to capitulate that drawback she looks to her sheep, not to the extended preparation of the wool after it is off the sheep's back.

I have emphasized this matter considerably because, although it concerns perhaps only a detail, it nevertheless shows significantly how we, prejudiced by our own practises, may take such things for granted and in doing so be quite mistaken in our conclusions. Such bias is often applied to much more important matters, and serious decisions concerning the treatment of natives are undertaken on the basis of obscure and vague information.

A minor process about which weavers disagree has to do with the strength of their fabrics. When I, emulating the weavers I had seen at work, used the batten to send home the weft, Marie was driven to one of her few vigorous protests. She and her mother do not depend on the batten for this purpose, but it has become a principle with them to use a heavy comb and take the impact on the thumb-joint. Their argument must be a good one. The use of the batten puts undue strain on the warp; the rug made with it is not as strong as one pounded entirely with the comb. Other women with whom I have discussed the question agree that the batten weakens the warp, but they use it nevertheless. This difference in native opinion is a matter of standards, an ideal put into practise. The fact that Maria Antonia and her daughters practise it is thoroughly consistent with their continued striving toward perfection. This is over and above the purely economic because no one knows their blankets have this quality and they are not paid more for them because of it.

I never talk about Navajo weaving to a group of laymen and rarely to an individual without being asked, "How long does it take to make a blanket?" I have tried to show in *Spider Woman*, my informal account of learning, that it is impossible to answer the question. Circumstances are so varied, interruptions are so numerous, work is so erratic, that time must be left out of the calculation. Great stress is laid on the economic value of weaving to the Navajo, and I think its value can hardly be emphasized. Yet, if the weavers had a conception of time remotely approaching ours and if they correlated with it a money value, there is not one who would feel satisfied with the monetary reward. Atlnaba could weave a small rug like that of Pl. XIV, *c* in a day if she kept at it, but that means a day of weaving alone. She could spin the weft yarn in a day, perhaps in less time, but it would take her at least a day to spin the warp. It is doubtful if she would finish it in that time. We have not counted carding in this estimate. Three days of close application is about the least a skilled and rapid worker like Atlnaba would need to complete even a small rug. At the time she made this one for me (summer of 1932 when prices were at the lowest) $2.50 or $3.00 would have been a good price.

It is, however, a mistake to estimate the weaving on this basis. Rarely, indeed, does a woman start in to weave a blanket and go through with it in the systematic way we presuppose. She needs warp, let us say, and her mother needs weft yarn, her sister has perhaps enough of each for a blanket half done, her niece helps everybody. They therefore have a carding party. All four get busy and card if they have that many pairs of towcards. If not, one or two spin while the others card. Thus they, within a few days, produce enough warp and weft to more than supply their immediate wants. A judicious worker calculates exactly how many skeins of dyed yarn she needs so as to have the color exact throughout, but she will be as careful not to have a great deal left over, for her next rug may demand different colors. Thus the different processes go on at varying rates of speed and when making an estimate as to the amount a woman earns a day, we must always remember that the weaving and related activities are not by any means the only thing she does. However, what is true for all handicrafts prevails: whatever the weaver gets, it is not really enough.

Handcraftsmanship must be reckoned not only in dollars and cents but also in satisfaction. There is something about making a beautiful object which cannot be measured tangibly. There is no doubt that the weavers feel this. I sincerely believe that Atlnaba and Maria Antonia would weave if they never received a cent for their blankets. Their artisanship is to them a pride and a joy. They try to get as much money as they can for it, but that is a matter distinct from their aesthetic reward.

I may cite a few examples of the most pretentious tapestries. Atlnaba worked nearly a year on the Sun's House tapestry. She was not well during the time and did not work steadily. On another much larger one, she worked a little over a year and received twice as much for it. Hastin Gani's Wife set up her last sandpainting blanket, fourteen feet square, almost the maximum size, exactly five weeks before she took it down completed. She had all of her yarn ready at this time. She had much help in carding and spinning from the womenfolk of her family, but no one could help much in the actual weaving because none but she knows how to design.

In contrast to this — a case more usual by far — is that of Atlnaba who has had a sandpainting on the loom for more than three years and it is still only a little more than half finished. She has been hindered by illness, her own and that of others, and by lack of help for the usual activities of the range. For not only is there no one to help her card and spin much — she really prefers to do her own — but the family has even had to hire assistance for the care of its large herds and that help is neither continuous nor dependable.

For special blankets of such size and intricacy as here described the weavers may receive as much as $750, or even more. It is impossible to give "standard prices" for any blankets because during the period of my learning there has been the greatest instability in values of all kinds. The general economic conditions have caused prices to vascillate from the highest to the lowest (1932) in this interval and I am unable to predict the average at which they may "settle".

This brings me to a consideration of the future of the Navajo blanket and the question of progress. It begins, according to our knowledge of it, as a fully developed product. We cannot attest to its rise. From an excellent beginning there has been degeneration along some lines, improvement along others. My summary would be one of general advance. The degeneration has come about through use of native wool. Except for the mohair (which is not of a high quality in a White market) the Navajo produce little, if any, yarn which can compare with the materials they first obtained from the Whites, bayeta, Saxonys and Germantowns. In my opinion, even the best yarn does not compare with that made by the Hopi and other neighboring Pueblos who evidently have a criterion of fineness in their cotton thread.

I think, however, that what the Navajo yarn lacks in fineness is more than compensated for by its character, a quality all its own. I can think of ways to improve it; I cannot be sure this character would be preserved. My suggestions are along the lines of more careful cleansing and dyeing. My "vegetable dye" blanket would, I think, be not a whit less attractive or desirable if I did not quite frequently have to pick a little stick or a burr out of the coarse yarn. Complete awareness of such foreign particles and frequent handling are the only ways in which this fault can be corrected; the most careful workers do correct it.

It is almost certain that purer colors could be achieved if the wool were washed before dyeing. With the introduction of the new, well-colored dyes encouragement might be given along this line as well. Water should not be so scarce as to make it necessary to skip the washing. The water-saving habit is so strongly rooted that the weavers tolerate the omission of initial washing and subsequent rinsing. They are, however, keenly aware of the fact that such additional processes would greatly improve their webs. The solution of this particular question is not in the hands of the weaver alone. It is the eternal problem of getting "little drops of water on little grains of sand", one which has vexed the Navajo as long as they have sojourned in this desert land and one which will doubtless vex them and their white friends and helpers for many a year to come.

I have already expressed my sentiments on dyes and color. I believe there will be a great improvement in these matters, that time, competition, and emulation will do the rest, so that colors and combinations will become constantly more pleasing. I would here recapitulate my emphasis on the encouragement of matching, especially of carrying strands over a wide space if there is danger of mis-matching. This remark is gratuitous; the traders have been, and are, constantly scolding about this very matter.

There is no doubt that from the point of view of technical control and elaboration of design the Navajo have made unbelievable strides. In these matters, I should advise leaving them to their own devices and tastes. We have nothing to teach them. I should like to give one final faint yelp against encouragement of sandpaintings in weaving.

In this I am on the side of the most obstinate of the old orthodox medicine-men. My reasons are different from theirs but I do not believe that in the end the result is worth the emotional price the weavers pay even if money did not enter in. Besides this my reason is personal taste; I don't *like* the sandpainting tapestries. I do not expect this unreasonableness or my taste to influence the Navajo blanket by one jot or tittle.

There is in my opinion one factor besides color which might eliminate some of the monstrosities we now see and cause the production of more of the better blankets. That is the use of the blanket by the Navajo himself. It will be remembered that those he uses, chiefly as saddleblankets, are among the best artistically. That is, the proportion of good saddleblankets to all saddleblankets made, is far above the ratio of good blankets to all those made. It is not likely that the Navajo will take to wearing his own blanket, although he pays large sums for the Pendletons he and his women wear. During the lean days his characteristic philosophy was, "We don't get anything for the sheep, but we can at least eat them and the women can weave the wool." But the business depression in the outside world has showered millions of dollars of Government money onto Navajo shoulders, and it does not seem likely that he will follow out his logic.

XXI How to buy a Blanket

It is not difficult to become a judge of value of modern Navajo blankets. The visitor to a trading post which has a wide choice can best test the standards, because he will see all varieties of weave, from the worst to the best, from the finest to the coarsest. The first test of a good rug is its straightness. It should lie flat on the floor and its edge should be even. One must not expect perfection, however, for hardly any rug is perfect, but flatness and relative evenness of width are desirable above all things.

After inspecting the edge, the buyer should hold the rug against the light. If the weaver was successful with her edge, it is more than likely that her web is good. When held up to the light, it should be even in thickness and the lines of weaving should look straight. The uniformity of the weave depends upon well-spun yarn. The lines of weft also depend upon the yarn, but even with excellent yarn, may be skewed by the weaving. The inspector will doubtless detect diagonal rows of small holes at certain places. These are not due to faults, but to the way in which the Navajo weaver builds up her fabric (see p. 90), and if well handled (if the holes are regularly spaced and small) are not to be counted against the value of the rug. If the blanket is more than three feet long, the buyer testing the rugs may find a kind of ridge with holes made by stitches and pressure halfway up the rug or perhaps even twice across it at intervals of about a third its length. These he is not to hold against rug or weaver. As the Navajo weaving is organized today, there is no prospect of eliminating these marks which are due to the fact that the weaver sews a part of her weaving down so that she can reach the rest of it (see p. 81). I would advise the prospective buyer to go over a number of rugs testing his judgment on edge and excellence of weaving. He might lay them out in what he judges to be the order of perfection, and the traders I know will be glad to instruct him if he is wrong.

Let us suppose he has set for himself a general criterion of value by examining the qualities of several rugs. He will next want to choose some for himself. This choice will depend upon many things: How much is he willing to pay? What does he wish to use the rug for? What colors does he like or need? What kind of designs?

The price of blankets varies according to fineness and uniformity of weave and size. Those are the two standards considered by the trader in buying. It is impossible even to summarize the prices at which Navajo rugs may be purchased, for the prices vary greatly depending on the time and the place. The price changes with the price of wool in the wholesale market, but there are other factors, not always determinable, which control it.

There is a Navajo rug or blanket for almost every purpose. They are made in the form of pillow tops, runners, rugs for the floor varying from the smallest to gigantic pieces. There are soft webs of fine weave which would do well for table runners, or larger, for bed or couch covers. They are useful as automobile, beach or camping robes, and many make attractive wall hangings.

Most buyers know and like the rugs having some red. More rugs with black, white, gray and red are sold than of any other combination of colors, and these are the best known. Many other colors are utilized and liked, too, and the final choice depends on the buyer's taste which, as I have said before, is versatile. Many, however, will pass by the saddle-blanket weaves and the blankets in vegetable dyes. In so doing they are likely to miss a great deal, as they do also in passing over the rugs which do not contain red. None of these is, as is often said, "un-Navajo". In each class they are really Navajo in following the most ancient tradition.

Besides being of traditional color and pattern, they have an added value, for among them may be found specimens which are suitable to elaborate housefurnishings, especially if such furnishings are of simple design or have a tendency toward modernism. A red blanket may be gaudy and handsome, but it may not compare in style with one executed in black and white with a touch of gray here and there. The black and white one would fit in where the red could never be used. The modern vegetable dye rugs and blankets may be found to blend in with any color scheme. They contain soft purples, pink or rose, greens, blues and yellows with emphasis on any color one may wish.

The design, as well as the colors chosen, must depend upon the person choosing the rug. One will choose a broad sweeping design, another a surface covered with many small patterns with greater or less degree of unity; all are for the buyer's enjoyment and there are no rules for him to follow. He "knows what he likes". For the extension of his own experience and knowledge I request him to inspect the more unusual weaves and colors often, even though at first he may not think them typical. For if his interest grows, as it can hardly help doing, he will derive great enjoyment from them, the result of craftsmanship and skill. He may even advance so far that he will choose for his own, instead of looking askance, a saddleblanket with a design completed in half the space and an entirely different one in the other half. When he does this he is *almost* a connoisseur.

These remarks all point to ideals. It is not common to find the highest ideals all apparent in the same piece. One which has excellent design and color will have a crooked edge; one which has a good edge will have an excellent design but the colors will be impossible. Then one will turn up which has color, design, style! The shopper will be attracted to it beyond all the others. This rug will become "it" to him, and if he does not buy it he will always remember it and be sorry. The edge will be reasonably well done but the weaving is coarse though even. The wise buyer will choose this for his own because he really likes it, and at the same time knows its shortcomings. He does not like it because of them but in spite of them, and his choice is not the result of ignorance.

I would warn a buyer against a snare which might cause him considerable disappointment. That is, ordering a blanket "just like another". I have never seen a modern Navajo imitation of any blanket that was an exact replica. Sometimes the hoped-for imitation is far better than the original; it is in more cases than not, very different. This circumstance is not very different from our own experience. I give a dressmaker a beret to copy and what I get back shows little relation to the pattern I gave her. Unlike the Navajo, the new is rarely an improvement on the old.

We are sometimes asked by persons who cannot select their purchases from the large stocks of the Navajo blanket dealer, how they are to distinguish a Navajo from some other kind of blanket. Those from the Southwest, and Central American region are the only ones I know which have the *same* design on *both sides*. All other types having one color on one side have a different color on the opposite side at the same point. This is true of only the special weaves (see p. 99) of the Navajo which rarely appear in a general market and which must be learned. Navajo rugs may usually be distinguished from others by their designs. A few old blankets of Hopi, Zuñi and Navajo might be undeterminable, but they concern the buyer infrequently. Besides, the value of all three kinds would he about equal.

I do not think categorical instructions can be given about old blankets upon which high values may be set. Even appraisers and connoisseurs differ greatly in their evaluations, and it is better for the novice to consult an expert who is not selling the piece before he buys. In this connection it may be well to add a warning against blanket "stories". Many stories of blankets are told; they carry more weight and are more fascinating to the inexperienced buyer than they are when he of necessity must liquidate his investment and himself becomes the seller. A word to him who is wise enough to acknowledge his ignorance and inexperience in the blanket field is: to suspect stories which are sensational or thrilling, particularly indefinite tales of great age which cannot be corroborated by persons with no interest in selling, and those regarding the three, four, or five years it took a woman to weave a blanket. The answer to the last is that, although the woman had it on her loom that long, she simply was not working at it (cp. the speed of Hastin Gani's Wife, p. 60).

XXII *Virtuosity*

One of the most astonishing impressions one gets of Navajo activity, although it is always superficially simple, is that it is thoroughly worked out and unusually complete. I cannot refrain from making a few general remarks about what I consider "the virtuosity of Navajo life". It is not peculiar to the Navajo, but rather to all people I know who do not have many "things". It is difficult, almost impossible, for us to understand how life can be defined in such "low terms". The reason for our lack of comprehension is that each one of us has a technique of living based upon only the most restricted knowledge and experience of our own environment. We use, more frequently abuse, the many machines upon which we lay our hands from day to day. We know little about their proper use, less about their care, next to nothing about their manufacture, and nothing at all about their replacement. This is particularly true of city dwellers. Country people know how to do more kinds of things but they generally know as little about machinery.

It is with surprise, then, that one observes a people, whose every individual has a reasonably broad knowledge of his entire culture. I have never ceased to wonder at the casualness with which life is carried on by the Navajo. The matter-of-factness with which they meet emergencies stipulates not only great resourcefulness but also perfect virtuosity, a control of the factors which go to make up different phases of life. Above all, it involves a state of mind, which once attained, is a comfortable possession. When I first went to the Navajo country I used to worry, as do all new-comers, about this and that. I have now adopted the confidence the Navajo have in themselves which may perhaps be formulated, "If it is worth doing, we can do it, if it is not — and our inability to do it may prove it is not — what does it matter anyway?"

This confidence has its roots in self-reliance, resourcefulness and rationalization of a bad situation. It is the spirit, not only of the pioneer, but also of all those who have had to make much out of little. It defines the difference between the old West and the East, between colonies and a mother country.

Navajo weaving is one example of many which illustrate the impression. I know of only one region where good weaving is done in a fashion cruder than that of the Navajo. It is the northern part of the Northwest Coast where the elaborate Chilkat blankets were made with only a finger twining technique. Not even a loom to fasten down the warps, no device at all to separate the sheds. But even the crude manner of Navajo weaving is surprising in its results to the uninitiate (I may say even to the initiate!). For, although the loom is the simplest combination of unfinished sticks (the more unfinished, the more efficient they are in some respects!) and miscellaneous looking strings, it lacks, nevertheless, nothing which is essential.

It matters not that the machine is smaller, not that it is hand operated. The fundamentals are: means for shedding, for laying in weft, for beating it, for holding and tightening the warp, and a device for removing the finished part of the web. These are all present in the Navajo loom, though each one is hand operated. All additions used on other loom types, no matter how large or complicated, are refinements, not essentials. Each part of the Navajo loom is produced on the Reservation. True, at the present time, balewire, that humble and indispensable servant of any man who does more than pass through the Southwest by train, may be used in erecting the loom-frame and in fastening the loom to the frame. But if a Navajo has no balewire, she twists herself some strong string which does quite as well. Indeed, she often prefers it. It may be that the same weaver may use an umbrella rod for a heald or a rib for a shuttle, or even a sacking-needle to finish off her blanket. But if she does not have one, she can make out quite as well with her assortment of reeds. She substitutes in such case patience and dexterity for iron.

If our weaver lives in a wooded locality, her husband cuts the loom parts from his own range. Natural roughness of the four pieces of the loomframe is a great advantage. At Red Point's I never have any trouble with wires and strings slipping. At home where my loom, made by a German cabinet-maker, is smoothed and finished according to the least of his ideals, my strings, particularly the rope that tightens the warp, are constantly slipping. I have been compelled to rub the rope with rosin; it is now only reasonably satisfactory. If the Navajo weaver lives on a dull barren plain, her husband will journey to the mountains for the parts of the loomframe. This will involve a trip in the wagon and perhaps the whole family will have an outing.

The weaver may live on the mountain. If that is the case, there may be plenty of hard oak near her home and her husband, father, or son will fashion combs and battens of all sizes from it. She or they will have a surplus supply which they may give to relatives or friends less favorably situated. The old warp spinner will trade warp for a new batten or for a fresh supply of reeds necessary to every good weaver's kit. Even dyes may be produced from the natural supply of vegetation and minerals. One tool only which the weaver uses she must buy, her towcards.

To a degree the Navajo is independent in his food supply, but growing trade with Whites has given him artifical needs he cannot himself fulfill. He eats a great deal of wheat bread, although the amount of wheat he himself produces is small. In the old days corn took its place and even now corn, cooked in many forms, plays a large part in the diet. If a party of unexpected visitors arrives, the women casually go out, kill and butcher a sheep or a goat, even as our grandmothers used to kill chickens or squabs in a similar emergency. A prosperous family trades in large quantities so it is likely to have flour, coffee and sugar on hand and it is not long before a respectable

Navajo meal may be served. The hostess thinks no more of getting her meat supply from her flock than our own hostess does of sending out, or phoning to the delicatessen.

There are few Navajo activities, other than weaving, in which the Navajo is independent of supply from Whites, but when mishaps occur, he shows control of the situation which is as matter-of-fact as his daily life. One day at the well I neglected to tie a knot properly and our only good bucket fell to the bottom. Marie laughed and sent a child to a house in sight for a long hooked wire. After Marie had fished up the bucket and we had finished our work, the car was caught in dry quicksands. With the aid of some men who came to the well we worked for three hours before we got out, but at no time was there a dearth of ideas as to *how* to work.

In this case, as in many others, rain was the cause of considerable inconvenience. When the first shower beats down upon a house, there is no telling where it will leak. The Navajo folds himself into small compass and sits still until the shower is over. He then busies himself about mending the roof and the chances are that the next rain, if not too severe, will find him prepared and his house snug. A small brook may threaten to break into the house while the shower is on. He (or she, the women know how to do all a man does) then takes off his moccasins and stockings, grasps a shovel and digs a ditch to divert the water from the dwelling. If it catches the house-keeper unaware, she may see her cooking utensils floating about on the surface of a temporary lake inside her house. She does not like it, but makes the best of it. She knows the rain will not last forever; she has nothing it can permanently damage.

A foresighted white observer might say, "But why don't they do those things *before* it rains?" The answer is, "You can't tell where the house leaks until it rains." After it is once mended it takes a heavy downpour, indeed, to break through a well-made roof. As for the ditch, there is usually some slight channel for the water to take near a dwelling, but no one can predict exactly which direction the water is coming from until it arrives. There are, of course, many Navajo who leave all these things until the last minute but even they know how to handle an emergency.

The Navajo has a different idea of comfort from ours, but according to his lights he can make himself and his companions comfortable with very little. One thing always included in the "very little" is fire. If one is wet or cold, he needs a fire; if the weather is balmy and fair, he needs a fire to cook his humble meal. Perhaps the conditions are pleasant; the wind is warm and he has no food; then especially he needs a fire for company.

A good husband and a conscientious son-in-law see to it that there is plenty of wood on hand, although rarely is there enough chopped ahead of time for even one fire. When the heavy rains of midsummer come, the problem of starting a fire may be important. There are many simple ways. It may be lighted under a tree if only the ground is wet. Soft dry bark, torn from the protecting overhanging trunk of a juniper may be used as tinder, small sticks torn from the heart of the juniper wood will give enough of a flame to ignite the heavier wood eventually.

If the shower has been so severe as to soak the bark and all parts of the tree, resin picked from the branches of the piñon will serve. If, however, there is a sedentary group as there was at Red Point's, the fire will be borrowed. A shovelful of glowing coals taken from the nicely functioning fire of one house is sufficient nucleus to start even a pile of thick, wet sticks to flaming in no time. Where wood is abundant, as in the mountains, a whole tree may be dragged to the campfire. It is pushed up into the fire as it gradually burns away. Another method is to start the fire about the base of a dead tree trunk. We once had a burning pillar of this kind for a campfire, but when we turned in the Navajo guide put it out remarking as he did so, "Somebody else might like to use what is left". It is my impression, however, that the Navajo are not generally as conservationistic or altruistic as this.

A necessary part of Navajo family life is a wagon. The only limit the Navajo puts on the load he carries over the rough roads he travels is that set by the nature and age of the vehicle. So it is not an unusual sight to find on the road, at perhaps the only crossing of a sharp wash, a broken down wagon. The owner will not, however, be off begging for help. The chances are he will be working on the broken part right there. He may digress from his labor to unload the wagon so your auto can pass, or he may set about helping to shovel away the bank on either side so you can manage to go on. If you also get stuck, he will not desist until he has helped you out. He and his party will push; if that does not suffice, he will hitch his horses to the car. All these interruptions for which he may be responsible, and the ensuing labor, he bears with a joke and a smile and a readiness to make the best of the situation.

Once when I was driving from Ganado on a main highway, I came upon a similar sight written in automobile terms. A Navajo, driving a truck, had been halted by a broken gear. He was about two miles from a white settlement, so he had set about locating and remedying the trouble. When I arrived he had tools and car parts so spread over the wide road that there was no possibility of passing. I stopped and was pleased to note that he talked Navajo to me as if I were born to the tongue. He indicated casually that his trouble involved taking out the axle and, as he had no wheel-puller, it was necessary to take the wheel along with the axle. He finally got these parts detached from the car but not from each other. Carefully nursing the machinery in his lap he sat, erect as he would on his horse, in the back seat of the Ford as I drove him back to Ganado. He had not expected exactly this kind of luck, but he had worked vigorously in the expectation that someone would help him out.

At another time my own car took fire on the way to Gallup. I was able to put out the fire but did not know what to do next. A truck driven by a Navajo pulled up and the driver disconnected the unruly wire, bound it up with electrical tape and we both went blithely on our respective ways. Ten years ago, when I first went into the Navajo country, few of them had automobiles and those who had were poor drivers and did not know how to take care of the cars. Today many of them have cars and some are skilful at repairing them temporarily or at fashioning a makeshift. They apply their native experience to the task of making something out of nothing, a hammer from a rock, a spring block of a piece of wood, an engine-hanger out of balewire. The greatest comfort in their country is the thought that, no matter how bad the breakdown, the load never remains on the road or in the ditch indefinitely; all mishaps are cleared up sooner or later with the help of Navajo and white inhabitants.

The easy disposition of the Navajo is remarked by all who have contact with him. There is no better exemplification of it than his participation in sports. He is a good sport in games or in life, and by that I mean, of course, that he is a good loser. He meets defeat in everyday exertions, such as drought, tornado, heavy snow, flood, with the same philosophy as the loss of a valuable bracelet in gambling. He has set his stakes, played the game; he has lost. He pulls his belt a notch tighter and starts off a poorer but a wiser man. He likes to have more, but he can make out with less.

The Navajo is not a busybody. Unless you quite definitely place upon him a given responsibility, he will allow you to go into danger, even to death, without interference, but ask his advice and he will give it freely and honestly. You will find also that it will be the part of wisdom to take it, especially if it concerns roads, water, or anything that relates to his own kind of life. His aloofness about your welfare may be highly exasperating. When we came back from the Snake Dance one time, we started after dark, we had seventy-two miles to go, a storm threatened ahead of us, we had a two-month's-old baby, and we were all tired. There was every reason in the world that we should avoid delay.

The women may respect my aptness at weaving but the men can have nothing but scorn for my stupidity about trails. I am bad enough in the daytime but at night I am hopeless. This night our route lay directly east. Shortly after we passed Keam's Cañon we seemed to be going directly toward a natural light, clouded but definite. It puzzled me and I finally remarked. "There is no moon tonight. What is that light?"

"It's the sun setting," answered Tom calmly.

"The sun setting!" said I scornfully. "Why, we're not going west, we should be going east!"

"We're on the wrong road," he said, "ever since we passed that sign back there." I argued, I must confess with little conviction, rather to dispel my aggravation. Red Point upon consultation corroborated Tom's statement and we drove back two miles to "that sign back there" where we found an obscure one pointing out our way.

There are some situations beyond the Navajo's practical control. They include illness and such misfortunes as may be brought on by fate. In circumstances like these he needs supernatural assistance. He has a way of invoking the aid of the gods and a carefully stipulated method of applying it when given. His implicit belief in it makes his ritual often successful.

In those cases where it fails and the individual concerned dies, he brings forth once more the fatalism upon which his existence is based. One summer I left Ganado just before Red Point was to sing the Shooting Chant for a man who lived nearby. Several months later I received a letter from one of my interpreters in which he remarked in the characteristic Navajo way, "Red Point didn't sing the Shooting Chant after you left. The man died, that's the reason. We were all very sad about it, but as I told the family, 'We have plenty to do to take care of the living, we must not worry about the dead'."

Appendices

Appendix I. Implements and Materials for Rugs

It will be necessary for the learner, to have a full set of tools and materials ready before beginning to work. They have all been mentioned in the body of this work as the various steps in the weaving process were taken up. It may, however, be convenient to have a full list of the most important necessities and one follows. The items are mentioned in the order in which they are used:

1. One pair towcards (available at most trading posts for about $ 1.25). This is for the preparation of the wool (Chapter II).

2. One spindle. For spinning and twisting of the yarn (Chapter III and Lessons 2—5).

3. Dyes: as many packages as there are colors other than white, gray, or natural sheep brown (Chapter IV and I).

4. Round sticks: at least three, about one inch in diameter, two of them as long as the blanket is wide, one somewhat longer. Broomsticks are ideal. Used in stringing warp and in constructing loom (Chapters VII and VIII).

5. Reeds, about one-quarter to three-eighths inch in diameter; at least two for ordinary weaving, four for the diagonal weaves, to serve as heald rods. It is best to have many of these for they dry out and break easily. Then too, they should be graduated in size, thinner ones being better for the work as it gets tight when nearing completion. A straight piece of balewire may be the last heald (Chapters VII, VIII, and IX).

6. Battens: a whole set, the largest three inches wide, and three or four others each gradually becoming smaller until the last is only half an inch or less wide. Add to these a set of reeds of small diameter (not more than one-eighth inch), each one of which has a flat end, smoothed down by shaving and use. For weaving, see Chaps. IX, X.

7. Combs: a set also of graduated sizes, beginning with a broad heavy comb, and ending with a slim narrow one. Three or four are sufficient, two would do, a large and a small. See Chaps. IX, X.

8. Reeds: about one-eighth inch in diameter not specially smooth and with naturally broken ends. Three or four of these to serve as shuttles for large expanses of self-weaving. See Chaps. IX, X.

9. Sacking-needles: several of different sizes. If only one, let it be small or not more than medium in size. See Chap. X.

If large rugs are to be woven, the size of the sticks which hold warps and of everything except battens and combs must be proportionately larger. There is a natural limit to the size of the reeds used for healds, four feet let us say. The shortness is overcome by using two or more across the wide rug. One is not able to weave a space four feet across at a sitting anyway so it will not matter that more than one rod is used to form a shed. The chief difference between the small and large rugs lies in the manipulation of the loom parts.

The weaver will have her kit with her whenever she sets about weaving. The tools not in use will lie handy behind the loom ready at a moment's notice to be pressed into service.

The following materials are necessary for the blanket:

10. One ball warp, large or small according to the size of the blanket. The color makes no difference, for in a properly woven rug the warp does not show.

11. Four to six hanks yarn of different colors, the number and colors depending upon the size and pattern to be woven. This is the weft yarn. The worker should be sure when dyeing it to dye enough of each color to finish the rug. It is difficult, almost impossible, to match colors perfectly in home dyeing, even our most expert silk manufacturers fail to do so.

12. A quantity of coarse string, two-, three-, or four-ply, at least somewhat more than four times the width and four times the length of the blanket. Each length and width should be in a single piece. This is to be used as end twining and as edge. By carefully selecting the colors and combinations of end and edge strands great subtlety may be secured. Not much of the edge shows, but that which does gives a fine air of thoughtful finish. Next to the consideration of quality and quantity of warp the Navajo weaver estimates carefully the amount and color of her edge cords.

13. Lengths of strong string (from six to nine inches) for various tying purposes. It may be two- or three-ply; mohair makes the strongest.

14. Balewire.

15. A large quantity of medium weight smooth cord. For making heald loops. See Chap. VIII.

16. A long strong heavy rope (mohair is best, clothesline is excellent, especially after use). This become the tension cord. See Chap. VIII.

The items 10, 11, 12 will be used in the particular rug being made, 13-16 may be used again and again. They will become ever shorter and weaker but may be pieced and reinforced indefinitely. New pieces of string and rope will be used for the larger rugs, the used ones will be unobtrusively delegated to smaller ones. Everything used must be above all strong. Strength may be attained by tightness of spinning and doubling or tripling the ply of the cord. Bear in mind always that the strain on every thread is tremendous and that the whole web is only as strong as the weakest thread.

Appendix II. Implements and Materials for Warp Weaving

1. Germantown yarn, red and green.
2. 1 ball of grocer's twine.
3. Spindle, same as for rug.
4. For long wide belt: two poles a foot or two longer than one-half complete length including fringe.
5. Two crosspoles: used with No. 4 for large belt, used with belt strap for narrower bands, one, if attached to a support at one end and to weaver's belt at the other.
6. Strong string with which to tie crosspoles to uprights.
7. 4 round sticks 4-6 inches long, not more than ½ inch in diameter, thinner if for small bands, 2 used for separating warp-loops, 2 for harness.
8. 1 short (about 4 inches long) flat smooth stick, used for subsidiary heald rod.
9. A short clublike batten.
10. A small smooth stick to serve as shuttle upon which weft-cord is wound.

Appendix III. Lessons

Lesson 1. Carding

Grasp the towcards firmly, one in each hand as in Pl. II, *a*. With a small wad of wool placed on the lower card (held in the left hand), draw the upper one firmly over the lower several times. The staple of the wool will begin to lie more evenly and there will be a tendency for the wool to lie more thickly at the center or end of the cards. It may be brought to lie evenly along their surface by drawing the card held by the left hand over the one in the right hand as in Pl. II, *b*. The carding continues by repeating these motions: by means of right-hand card draw wool through teeth of left-hand card, remove wool from between teeth by reversing direction of one card, rearrange on cards by pulling one over the other.

As the staple gradually comes to lie so that all its parts are in the same direction, the wool will become cleaner. Large quantities of sand, burrs, and other objectionable particles will fall out or be picked out by the worker. Finally she will judge that the wool is in the proper stage for efficient spinning and by combining the two motions described, she will lift the lap from the teeth first of this card, then of that, so that the two fluffy wedges lie with their thin sides overlapping. The experienced carder will have a light pad of wool of an exact rectangular shape.[1]

The Europeans use their towcards so that a short roll results. They take a much smaller wad of wool between the cards, do not draw the fibers out nearly as long, and after they all lie in one direction, manipulate the upper card over the lower so that the wool takes on the rope shape. The Navajo substitute an extra spinning for this procedure. It does not take nearly as long to form a Navajo rectangular carded lap as it does to roll the European roll into shape. I do not know if the time taken by the Navajo carding and first spinning is equal to that used by the Whites in carding the rope or not. To me the Navajo method seems more efficient; perhaps only because it is the way I learned.

Lesson 2. *Spinning*

The illustrations Pls. II, III will help the learner more perhaps than verbal directions, but several additional hints may be useful in avoiding pitfalls and discouragement.

Even though the spinner become as adept as Atlnaba, she will always find uneven portions in her roll of wool, particularly at the second twisting of her finished yarn. A constriction will mark off a portion of the wool at each end so tightly that for an inch more or less, there will be no chance for the intervening wool to twist. You will then rest the spindle on the thigh and use both hands to correct the unevenness Pl. II, e. This is done by grasping the yarn firmly between thumb and forefinger of the right hand, palm upward, and the thumb and forefinger of the left hand, the palm of which is turned upward. The left hand is in exactly the same position as when spinning. With the right hand untwist the yarn at the points where it was

[1] Not in a "thick, fluffy rope" as described by Amsden, p. 36. The ropelike appearance of his Pl. 13 is due to the first manipulation of spinning.

[206]

spun too tightly. Then with both hands pull out the fibers which have been caught between the two twists firmly but steadily. You may stretch them amazingly but you must be careful to do so in the right direction, that is along the line of the staple.

When the lumpiness has thus been pulled into circulation again, spin once more as usual and at this place the yarn will have the same thickness as it has elsewhere. The pulling of the fibers in order to make the yarn regular is a habit which Atlnaba never leaves off. If she is sitting near watching me work, she seizes a piece of yarn and pulls on it making it always more even than it was. When she is weaving she often does the same thing to her own yarn before she lays it in. Uniformly spun yarn makes for good texture; it makes weaving doubly easy for it lessens the need for evening up the rows.

In spite of all care there will remain on the wool of the beginner some fibers like thick fuzz which seem to have no connection with the main thread. There is nothing to do with these tufts but pull them off. They will not be present on the yarn of the expert.

The motion of the left hand in spinning weft is a loose twisting pressure of the thumb on the forefinger at the same time that friction between the two is pulling along the line of the staple from the spindle. The method of spinning warp is slightly different (Pl III, b). The loose twist is held quite tightly between thumb and forefinger and there is, instead of the stretching through a long distance, a lively twisting motion between thumb and forefinger. The distance between left hand and spindle is shorter than for weft and the spindle is revolved much faster. The emphasis in this case is on tightness and hardness of twist. I found I had very little trouble spinning warp if I picked up the spindle of an expert whose initial loose twist was even. I have the greatest difficulty in getting the first thick strand even. So far mine would not make good warp. But I cannot be discouraged when I contrast the small amount of time I have spent spinning with Marie's nine years of steady practise until she attained perfection.

Lesson 3. Twisting double-ply cord

Although the Navajo never use more than single-ply yarn nowadays in the main body of the weaving, they nevertheless know how to make multiple plies and use them for binding strings at sides and ends and for many other purposes. Such cord is of the greatest importance because many a good weaver gives special thought to her edge cords. She takes pride also in the kinds of cords and ropes she uses for tying and looping the parts of her loom.

Double-ply cord is made by laying the desired amount of warp yarn out on the floor in two diverging curly masses. Take a strand from each mass and wind the two strands over the fingers of the left hand holding the end tightly so the wound part will not curl and tangle. The spindle will be used in reversed position for all more-than-one-ply yarn or cord. Fasten the end of each of the two warp threads to be twisted at the right end of the spindle whorl, wrap the two strands, treating them now as one, twice around the short end of the spindle and roll on the thigh away from you as in Pl. III, *c*. The yarn is fed from the tight loops around the four fingers of the left hand to the spindle which quickly takes it up. The retwisted two-ply cord is wound on the long end of the spindle-stick near the whorl, just as it is for single-ply yarn.

Lesson 4. Triple-ply cord

To make three-ply cord, double the end of your warp ball for two or three inches and hold between your left thumb and forefinger. Then with your right thumb and middle finger within the loop grasp the warp and pull it through the loop as in Pl. III, *d*. Pull this loop to the length of the first one and again pull the long thread through the last loop. You will see now that you have a three-strand set of loops. As you continue the looping, the simplest sort of cat's cradle or string figure really, you will wind the loose three-strand arrangement firmly about the four fingers of your left hand. When you have the desired length, spin it over the short end of the spindle as you did for two-ply.

Lesson 5. Four- and more-ply cord

Four-ply cord is sometimes used. It may be made by doubling the two-ply, or combining the result of the three-ply cat's-cradle with an extra strand by means of spinning. I have never seen more than four-ply cord but it could be made easily by using various combinations according to the directions given.

Lesson 6. Twining lower and upper edge

The worker, sitting at the end of the warpframe over which the warp has been stretched, holds in her left hand the doubled length of three-ply cord whose center she has indicated by a rather long loopknot. She holds the loopknot in her left hand and catches the end nearest her under the first warp, the other end falling loose and coming from behind the warp crosses the first end between the first and second warp and is carried under the second (Pl. IV, *b*, Fig. 4). The first end now has the position the second had previously and thus each one alternately twines under, and over each warp loop, crossing the other between each warp. In twining this edge the worker keeps her left hand under the twining cords where she regulates the tension and the twist of the one coming from above. The right hand moves with one of the strands catching it under each warp as it moves toward the right.

After the warp-stringer has the warp properly spread by means of this twining to the extent of a hand measure, she inserts a small splinter or pine needle to mark it, then pushes the warps close together on the cross stick at her left, and twines another hand-space of the warp. She continues the operation until the width of the rug is secured.

I had never fully understood the reason for measuring off this way until I strung up a blanket for myself. Upon this occasion I did not measure off the hand measures because each was immediately pushed up against the next one and it seemed to me there was no need to do it. But, upon undertaking the next step, I found that this is a method of keeping the warps even. I do not think the Navajo weaver *counts* the number of warps to a hand but I am sure she *judges* the number as accurately as she does the total number for the rug, or even more so. I did not subdivide my space and I found my warps unevenly spaced.

The worker next does the twining to control the width of the warp at the other end. Since the size of her hand measure is always the same and since her tension is likewise consistent, the width of the second end will be nearly the same as the first. However, if it happens not to be accurate, the worker will divide the remaining cord evenly between the warps, nor will she be satisfied until the width at both ends is exactly the same.

Lesson 7. Constructing the harness

The weaver passes her batten through one shed, turns it to horizontal, and withdraws one of the reeds. This reed is to be supported outside of all the warp strands. The worker holds a rod along the outside of the warp with her right hand. It will save trouble if this rod is at least six to twelve inches longer than the blanket is wide. In her left hand she holds a loose ball of

[*209*]

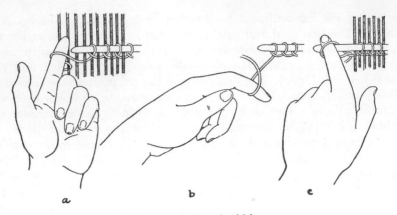

Fig. 34. Making heald loops

string. It should be smoothly and tightly spun but need not be strong or heavy. She turns her batten horizontally and carries one end of the string from left to right through the shed and fastens the end by means of a loose loop over the rod which now becomes a heald.

With her left forefinger she pulls the string between the first two warps which the batten holds forward at the right, turns it down so as to make a loop which she carries over the end of the rod she is holding in her right hand. The result is as in Fig. 34. It may take a little time to work out this loop, but any slowness the learner may encounter cannot be a quarter as exasperating as Marie's casual expertness. Her fingers fly so fast there is no way to tell, when they are in motion, how she achieves the loop. It is easy enough to work out when finished however.

Each warp held forward by the batten is caught into one of these loops and at the end the string is tied once more into a loop which is caught over the rod. The harness is now complete for the ordinary weave. There are two sheds, one formed by the heald and one kept in place by the heald rod. If the reeds used for healds are several inches longer than the width of the blanket, there will seldom be difficulty about them slipping out of the loops. They must of course be watched. There are times, such as when I worked with Mrs. Kinni's-Son, when the reeds are just as wide as the blanket or only an inch or two longer. In such a case the reed slips out of the loose loops so frequently as to become a nuisance. A thin string tied tightly around the reed at one end, carried through the center loop and tied as tightly around the reed at the other end will serve to keep the loops in place without further attention.

Lesson 8. Holding Batten and Comb

The position of batten and comb for the various operations is well shown by the illustrations. The change of the comb from the position of rest when the weaver is holding the batten to that of use when she is not is a simple one. The comb is held in practically the same way for both operations. At rest the third and little finger grasp it, and it lies teeth downward along the palm which is toward the weaver (Pl. V, *a*). When the batten is in horizontal position in the shed, the weaver slips her little finger to the other side of the comb so that it alone is under the comb, then she turns her hand so that her palm, instead of being toward her, is toward the ground. Three fingers instead of four curl about the comb handle, the comb which was in the same plane as the batten is now turned into one at right angles with it, and therefore with the warp. At first it may helpful to practise the swift change in position by itself when the mind is not occupied with all the other things that must be done.

Lesson 9. The Steps of Coördination

Since all the positions and motions of the hands are interrelated and since all are necessary at one time, or at least in such close succession that they can hardly be distinguished, I will enumerate them in outline form in their proper sequence. The outline may be thought of as related to Navajo weaving as a slow motion picture is related to a regular one:

1. Push heald rod close to heald loops — left hand.
2. Grasp batten in right hand.
3. Thrust batten into shed with right hand. The left hand may aid by lightly flipping the warps — in case their fibers adhere — or by holding a warp down firmly here and there. The left hand does not touch the batten.
4. Place proper edge strand over batten.
5. Grasp left end of batten with left hand, retain hold of right, and turn firmly to horizontal.
6. Lay weft in shed.
7. Pound down weft with comb.

8. Shift comb so that hand has batten position, grasp batten retaining comb in hand, and withdraw batten, sustaining position.

9. Push heald rod up — left hand. You have now finished one row through the shed regulated by the heald rod. The next process is a repetition of all the movements except that of shifting the healds.

1a. Pull heald firmly and evenly forward — left hand — so that all the warps it controls will be forward on batten.

1b. Flip back of fingers of right hand lightly over the warps.

Repeat 2—8 and start all over again.

Lesson 10. The Edge

It is necessary to take one strand of the two which form each edge on the end of the batten each time the weft is thrown across. The two strands of each edge are slightly twisted. Place the forefinger (right at right side, left at left) between them so that they have no twist at the bottom; then, with the thumb bring the inside one forward from the inside and place it over the batten. For about half an inch of weaving the weft should pass between the two edge cords in the same position. At regular intervals of that distance

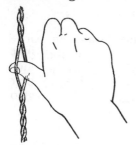

Fig. 35. Detail showing how to twist edge

— greater or less according to the fineness and style of the blanket — with the thumb bring the outside cord forward from the inside so that it crosses the cord at the inside and over the batten (Fig. 35). This operation will cause the edge strands to twist. The weft will be carried through the strands in this way for the same distance as before and they will again be twisted in the same way. The test of a blanket is its edge. If the edge strands are properly twisted at equal distances and if the width of the blanket is the same throughout, it is perfect.

The same method is used for the edge of the saddleblanket weaves, but the worker should remember that of the three or more strands hanging at the edge, the one she is to use should each time be inside the others.

Appendix IV. *Glossary of Foreign Terms*

Navajo	Scientific name	Common term	Part used
tcat'íní	Rumex hymenosepalum, occidentale	dock, sorrel (canaigre)	root
tsédokǫ́j		"rock-salt" soda-ash	mineral
kiłtsoi (łitsoi didjo·li)	Bígelovia	goldenrod	flower, stem and leaves
na'acdja'ilkéhí	Helenium Hoopesii	sneezeweed	flower
t'sa	?	sage	leaves
ha'altsadi	Juglans	walnut	shells and twigs
'awé t'sá·l	Cowania Mexicana	cliffrose	leaves and stems
t'cil hox^wé'é	Heuchera bracteata	Navajo tea	stems
tse'ésda·zí	Cercocarpus parvifolius	mountain mahogany	root bark
gad	Juniperus occidentalis	juniper	stems and leaves
gad ni'ełi		"cedar"	stems and leaves
kí·c	Alnus incana var. virescens	black alder	bark
ni' hadlá·d		one of the lichens	stems
hwoc ntye·li	Opuntia Missouriensis	prickly pear	ripe fruit
hwoc be'eldéhí	Senecio Douglasii	groundsel (spine brush, "cactus cleaner")	stem and flower or leaves
t'có		Colorado blue spruce	twigs
tádídí·n dot'łí·c	Delphinium scaposum	larkspur	petals
tsédidi	Mirabilis	four o'clock	petals
kį (tciłtcin)	Rhus aromatica, var. trilobata	aromatic sumac	twigs, leaves berries
t'cil dilɣésí tsoh	?	rabbitbrush	whole plant
dje·h			piñon gum

dle·c	montmorillonite	white clay	
da t'sa‧'	Phoradendron juniperinum (Engelm.)	mistletoe	plant

Appendix V. Glossary of Special Terms.

Batten, a stick about two or two and one-half feet long, broader than thick, used to make the shed and to pound down the weft.

Chant, see "sing".

Harness, the machinery which regulates the sheds, i. e., healds and heald rod, called also "rig".

Heald, one of the rods, or rods with loops which regulates the particular warps so as to make the shed.

Heald rod, the rod run under certain warps to make a shed. It needs no loops because it always regulates the topmost shed.

Heddle, same as heald.

Hogan, dome-shaped Navajo house.

Lock, the joining of two weft colors or strands.

Mordant, element in dye which makes it fast.

Sacking-needle, coarse curved needle used for sewing up sacks.

Sandpainting, elaborate mosaic made of colored sands, an important element of the "sing" and also of Navajo belief.

Shed, space between warp through which weft passes.

Sing, a rite sung for curing and success.

Vegetable dye, dye made from natural products, native plants and minerals.

Warp, yarn strung vertically, the foundation of weaving.

Warp-beam, the beam from which warp is delivered.

Web-beam, beam which carries off finished web.

Weft (woof), yarn used to weave horizontally.

Woof, same as "weft".

Yucca (yucca baccata), the soapweed, or Spanish bayonet, commonly seen in the Southwest country.

Bibliography

Amsden, Charles Avery. Navaho Weaving. The Fine Arts Press, Santa Ana, California, 1934.

— See Wyman.

Bartlett, Katharine. Why the Navajo came to Arizona. Museum of Northern Arizona Notes Vol. 5 (Dec., 1932): 29—32.

Colton, Mary Russell. Wool for our Indian Weavers — What shall it be? Ibid. Vol. 4 (June, 1932): 1—5.

Franciscan Fathers. An Ethnologic Dictionary of the Navaho Language. Saint Michael's, Arizona, 1910.

James, George Wharton. Indian Blankets and their Makers. A. C. McClurg & Co., Chicago, 1927. (Dover reprint).

Matthews, Washington. Navajo Weavers. Report Bureau of American Ethnology 3: 371—391.

— A two-faced Navaho Blanket. American Anthropologist n. s. 2 (1900): 638—642.

Orchard, William C. A Rare Salish Blanket. Leaflets of the Museum of the American Indian, Heye Foundation, No. 5, 1926.

Report of Commander General of the Interior Provinces of New Spain, 1786.

Spier, Leslie. Zuñi Weaving Technique. American Anthropologist 26 (1924): 64—85.

Wyman, Leland G. and Amsden, Charles. A Patchwork Cloak. The Masterkey Vol. VIII (1934): 133—137.

Index